GREAT FOLK INSTRUMENTS

to Make & Play

Dennis Waring

Sterling Publishing Co., Inc.   New York

A Sterling/Tamos Book

A Sterling/Tamos Book
© 1999 Dennis G. Waring

Sterling Publishing Co., Inc.
387 Park Avenue South
New York, NY 10016-8810

Tamos Books Inc.
300 Wales Avenue
Winnipeg, MB Canada R2M 2S9

10 9 8 7 6 5 4 3 2 1

Distributed in Canada by Sterling Publishing Co., Inc.
c/o Canadian Manda Group, One Atlantic Avenue, Suite 105
Toronto, Ontario, Canada M6K 3E7
Distributed in Great Britain and Europe by Chris Lloyd,
463 Ashley Road, Parkstone, Poole, Dorset, BH14 OAX, England
Distributed in Australia by Capricorn Lind (Australia) Pty Ltd.
P.O. Box 6651, Baulkham Hills, Business Centre, NSW 2153 Australia

Design A. O. Osen
Photography Dennis G. Waring and David Magnuson
Illlustrations Leo Simoens

Printed in China

Canadian Cataloging-in-Publication Data
Waring, Dennis, G. 1945–
        Great folk instruments to make & play
        "A Sterling/Tamos book."
        Includes index.
        ISBN 1-895569-43-5
1. Musical instruments--Construction. I. Title.
ML460.W279 1999   784.192'3   C99-920051-8

Library of Congress Cataloging-in-Publication Data
Waring, Dennis, 1945–
        Great folk instruments to make & play / Dennis Waring.
            p.   cm.
        Includes index.
        ISBN 1-895569-43-5
            1. Musical instruments--Construction. I. Waring, Dennis, 1945–
        Folk instruments. II. Title.
        ML460.W28 1999   99–31789
        784.192'3--dc21   CIP

CanadaWorkMark
Tamos Books Inc. acknowledges the financial support of the Government of
Canada through the Book Publishing Industry Development Program (BPIDP) for
our publishing activities.

NOTE If you prefer to work in metric measurements, to convert inches
to millimeters multiply by 25.4.

The advice and directions given in this book have been carefully
checked, prior to printing, by the Author as well as the Publisher.
Nevertheless, no guarantee can be given as to the project outcome due
to the possible differences in materials. Author and Publisher will not
be responsible for the results.

ISBN 1-895569-43-5

Table of Contents

INTRODUCTION

Making music is a pleasant and satisfying activity. For the music maker, sharing the experience with a friend or group of people creates a delight that rivals most other forms of communication. For the solitary performer, music is a satisfying way to express inner feelings and emotions. Music is both stimulating and cathartic. Its message transcends the barriers of language and culture to be shared by all people. No one really knows why music affects us the way it does, but the magic and empowerment that result from musical experience are universally undeniable. This book acknowledges the influences and charm of music and provides a way to increase your music-making pleasure through building the instruments that you play.

The construction and playing of musical instruments is not reserved for highly skilled craftsmen and musicians. It can be experienced by anyone who wishes to create their own sound-making devices. The scope of this book provides a variety of building projects and musical possibilities to satisfy children and adults. Even very young children can explore their innate interest in sound manipulation.

The instructions for building the instruments are detailed and easy to follow. Once the basic principles are mastered, however, it's easy to add variations and create your own designs. Many children are surprisingly skilled and enjoy making their own creative decisions.

In most cultures, music makers rely on their immediate environment to provide the means for building their musical devices. Gourds, bamboo groves, vines, and other natural materials have great potential. These are not as readily available in the urban environments of North America; however, we do have an endless assortment of plastic containers, discarded cans, piping, bottles, and other "junk" that can be recycled into instruments. Any local hardware store or lumberyard can provide the other materials and simple tools that are needed to get the building process under way.

This book contains building instructions for over 50 instruments. Detailed diagrams and photographs are included, as well as listings of required materials. The first section of the book contains guidelines for making and playing simple folk instruments. Directions for making more sophisticated instruments are found in the second section. These more complex forms of folk instruments require some specialized tools and hardware, but with conscientious preparation, time, and patience the experience is ultimately rewarding. Besides the pleasure it affords the hobbyist, instrument making can be a valuable educational tool for teachers of music, industrial arts, science, and ethnic studies. Instrument making provides hands-on experiences whereby children, and adults, can fully realize their creative and artistic talents.

Our environment is full of auditory impressions we call sounds. Most of them are so familiar that we do not consider their origin. But they are of incredible variety. High-pitched squeaks, low rumbles, loud crashes, soft rustlings make up the sound panorama that is constantly changing around us. There are a great many sound sources that allow us to actually feel and see (as well as hear) the movement that produces the sound. This movement is called "vibration." Some objects, however, vibrate so quickly or so slightly that the eye cannot perceive movement except with special devices. In all cases, however, the basic scientific fact is that vibration causes all sound.

When an object vibrates it sets the molecules in the air in motion much like the series of concentric waves created when a pebble is dropped into a body of water.

Sound waves travel at approximately 1,100 feet per second (which seems very fast until we think of light traveling at over 186,000 miles per second). When sound waves have enough strength to push the ear drum in and out, they are translated into neurological impulses that the brain perceives as sound. The lowest/slowest vibration humans can hear is about 20 cps (cycles per second, or sometimes called Hertz); the highest/fastest is around 20,000 cps. As we get older, this range may narrow because of "wear and tear" on the ears. It is good practice to always protect the ears from excessively loud sounds to preserve hearing sensitivity.

As you probably know, some form of energy is required to start anything moving, which means that energy is required to start the vibrations that result in sound. The more forceful the energy, the louder the sound. There are several ways to make objects vibrate: the more common types of energy include plucking, blowing, and striking. Bowing and shaking might also be included.

Some sounds are classified as "noise" and others as "musical." One way to differentiate the two is to try to sing the sound to yourself. If you can isolate a singable pitch, it will qualify as a musical note. A musical pitch has one dominant vibration in it with a definite number of vibrations per second; whereas, a noise is a jumble of mixed vibrations. Most musical instruments in this book produce definite notes and pitches, although there are a number of percussion instruments that rely on "controlled noise" for their special effect.

Instrument Organization

Classifying the world's musical instruments presents an interesting challenge for organologists (musical instrument scholars). Some instruments do not readily fit into usual string, wind, and percussion categories. The piano, for instance, is both a stringed and percussion instrument. To help clear up this confusion, academics have devised a system of classification that identifies what is actually vibrating. Thus, the terms chordophone, aerophone, membranophone, and idiophone were formulated. The prefix of these headings tells us that, respectively, the string, the air, the membrane, and the item itself are making the vibration or sound (phone). By this definition a piano is a chordophone instead of a membranophone or idiophone since the string is the source of the sound vibration. Can you classify other instruments using this system of instrument organization?

SIMPLE FOLK INSTRUMENTS
Chordophones

The historical record of most musical instruments is sketchy because of the perishable nature of instrument making materials. However, we do have references. One of the oldest has been left in the wall paintings in the caves of Les Trois Frères, France, (c 15,000 B.C). Many scholars believe that one particular wall painting depicts a shaman (dressed in bison garb) holding a musical bow against his mouth and performing a dance of enchantment with a real bison. This suggests that from the earliest days, instruments have been inseparable from ceremonial magic and supernatural ritual, and still have the power to induce mood change and enhance experience.

Another characteristic that modern stringed instruments share with their earlier counterparts is their primary components: strings and a resonator. The strings found on instruments such as the guitar, piano, harp, and violin are made of varieties of metal, nylon, sinew, and their combinations. Silk, twines, and plant fibers have been used in other cultures for the same purpose. How the strings are constructed (longer or thicker) is important to the kind of sound produced. Whether strings are tightly stretched or loose also affects their sounds. Consider the following three factors as a basic working guide.

1. Tension or tightness of the string affects the pitch: the tighter the string, the higher the pitch.
2. Length of the string also affects the pitch: the longer the string, the lower the pitch.
3. Thickness and material of the string affects pitch and tone quality: the thicker the string, the lower and fuller the sound.

Strings are activated by plucking with the fingers or plectrum made from a quill, bone, or plastic pick. The material used and the style of picking affects the tone produced. Another method of vibrating strings is striking them (piano) or bowing (violin). Bowing has been universally adopted, probably because of the sustained, voice-like sounds that result.

The sound produced is usually amplified, reinforced, and reflected by a hollow resonating chamber to which the strings are attached. In many cultures, gourds, calabash, hollowed logs, plant pods, bamboo tubes, sea shells, framed animal skins, and even human skulls have been used as resonating receptacles. In addition, constructed boxes of many configurations and sizes, such as the hourglass-shaped guitar, triangular balalaika, and pear-shaped lute, constitute a large and varied branch of the chordophone family.

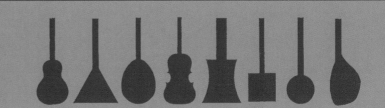

Tuning Mechanisms

Tuning mechanisms are one of the most important components on all stringed instruments. Tuning instructions for each of the instrument projects in this book focus primarily on a single type of mechanism; however, there are other options that may require modification of design. The design requirement regarding all tuners is that they must do two opposing tasks at the same time: hold tension but be turned or tensioned easily.

Screw Eyes

Screw eyes (wood screws with a loop on top) are the easiest and most inexpensive mechanisms for tuning simple stringed instruments. Choose a size that is big enough to turn easily and hold securely in the wood but small enough not to bump each other during the tuning process. They are not meant for long-term use because the wood will eventually cease to hold them under tension.

Materials
Wood screws
Instrument wire or string

Tools
Awl, nail, or drill bit

Procedure

1 Use an awl, nail, or drill bit (slightly smaller than the diameter of the screw eye) to start the hole.
2 Start turning the screw eye into the instrument, thread the string through the eye, and tie with a good tight knot, making sure string is moderately taut.
Note Screw eyes will turn easier if you put a nail through the eye and use it as a lever.

Tapered Dowels

Wood doweling is an alternative tuning material. Dowels are available at lumber stores, take a little more preparation, but look more attractive and provide better stability than screw-eye tuning.

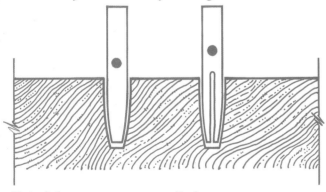

Materials
¼ to ⅜ in wood doweling
Instrument wire or string

Tools
Drill with appropriate bit
¹⁄₁₆ in bit for drilling string hole through dowel
Small saw (coping, dovetail)
Tapered rat-tail file
Sandpaper
Pliers or clothespin
Scissors

Assembly

1 Saw doweling into 2 in lengths.
2 Drill peg holes into instrument. Use tapered rat-tail file and taper hole by twisting file counterclockwise.
3 Whittle and sand one end of each peg to a slight taper and test in peg hole for a snug fit. Saw a slot ⅜ in long into end of peg so that it will compress and hold tension as it is twisted into peg hole.
4 With sandpaper flatten two sides on the end of peg opposite the tapered, slotted end and use pliers or clothespin to loosen or tighten strings. If you use larger tapered dowels, drill a hole in the end opposite the taper and insert a nail or smaller dowel to give leverage.
5 After fitting the peg to the hole, drill a ¹⁄₁₆ in string hole through the dowel just slightly above the top level of the board.
6 Thread string through hole, secure, and tighten. Trim excess string with scissors.

Wood Friction Pegs

Homemade whittled tuners look more authentic and will last much longer than screw eyes or dowels. Or use actual violin pegs purchased from most music stores.

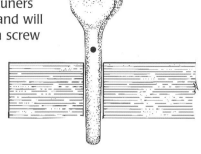

Materials
1 in x 3 in hardwood for each peg
Instrument wire or string

Tools
Coping saw or bandsaw
Vice or small C-clamp
Drill with $3/16$ in bit (for peg hole) and $1/16$ in bit (for string hole)
Rat-tail file, $3/16$ in diameter
Pocket knife
Sandpaper

Assembly

1 Draw chosen peg pattern on each piece of wood. Use one peg for each string.

2 Saw away excess wood.

3 Use pocket knife to carve shank of peg until tapered and round (diameter at small end should not exceed $3/16$ in).

4 Drill peg hole into instrument with $3/16$ in bit. Space holes evenly. Taper hole with rat-tail file.

5 Sand peg for snug fit (lubricate with soap or peg compound for easier turning, or rub with violin bow rosin for increased friction).

6 Put peg into hole and mark the spot where the string should go through the peg. Drill hole with $1/16$ in bit.

7 Carve large end of the peg and sand smooth.

Machine-Head Tuners

Perhaps the most efficient tuning mechanisms are those used on guitars, mandolins, and banjos. Inexpensive machine-head tuners can be found in most music stores while fancy, high-tech tuners are usually used on more sophisticated instruments.

Note Make sure thickness of peg head is thin enough so string hole pokes above top of board.

When using hardwood, pre-drill tiny holes slightly smaller than the screws which hold the tuners on or the tiny screws will strip or break.

Guitar tuners are geared to tighten the string slowly in relation to the amount of turning. They come in a variety of sizes and styles and should be acquired early in the building process to fit peg box or peg head. Inspect a factory-made classical and steel-string guitar to see how the tuners are accommodated. Tuners come singly or in units of three.

Banjo tuners come in a variety of styles, sizes, and price ranges. Some are geared and others work on the friction principle to hold the tension of the strings. Obtain tuners early in the building process and design peg head accordingly. Refer to factory-built banjos to see how tuners are installed.

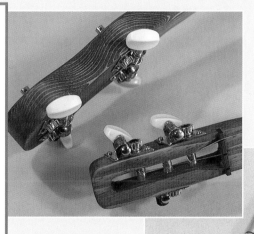

Machine-head tuners

Zither pins and tuning wrench

Zither Pins

Zither pins are used on autoharps, psalteries, hammered dulcimers, some harps, and pianos (larger size pin). They are excellent tuning mechanisms for some of the more complex multi-stringed instruments. Though generally standardized, zither pins may be found in different sizes, and care must be taken to make sure that the peg hole is slightly smaller than the pin so it will not slip under tension. A special key or tuning wrench is necessary to tighten and loosen the strings.

Musical Bows

MOUTH BOW

Among the various types of musical bows, the mouth bow is one of the oldest and most universal. This simple monochord in its many configurations is found throughout Africa, the Americas, and Asia, and is used to accompany song and dance. Old wall paintings in France show a bow being used in a musical posture (see p6) so it may have derived from a hunting bow. Africans and Brazilians use a gourd attached to the bow for enhancing resonance. In the United States it is said that the song bow of the Appalachian Mountains was adopted from the American Indians.

Materials

½ to ¾ in diameter tree branch or sapling, 3 to 3½ ft long (choose ash, maple, cherry, or birch), or wood yardstick or section of wood sawed from a board purchased from local lumberyard for bow

Steel guitar string (.022 wound string) or high-test nylon fishing line

Light or medium guitar pick, or length of thin wood dowel

Tools

Pocket knife, or drill with appropriate bit
Sandpaper

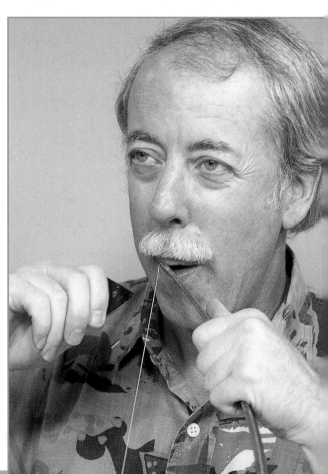

10

Assembly

1 If using a branch, trim off leaves and twigs. Peel off bark, if desired. If using a store-bought stick, trim and sand smooth.

2 Cut groove into each end 1 in from tip or drill a small hole through the branch at each end. Form a loop in the string to slip around the groove cut in the end or thread through drilled hole.

3 Bend branch while you secure the loose end of the string or wire at the opposite end.

To Play

1 Hold bow in left hand (if you are right-handed) about one-third down the bow.

2 Place small end against right cheek on outside of mouth.

3 Change pitch by moving tongue forward and back inside mouth and by changing size of opening of your mouth with the lips using the acoustic principle, as for the jew's harp. The string will produce one dominant drone that can be varied by changing mouth opening and arching tongue. Different pitches can be generated as well by slightly flexing the bow as you play to vary bowstring tension.

4 Hold good-sized pick in right hand and strum back and forth on string. Or you may tap the string with a light stick.

5 Option To change the fundamental pitch, add a tuning mechanism. Drill a hole in the large end of the stick and make a tuning peg. If you use a yardstick, a small knob of wood may be glued on one side and a friction peg or guitar tuner securely attached.

Compound musical bows are made by attaching several strings at different points along a rigid bow-shaped piece of wood.

A more dynamic sound can be achieved by attaching an open-ended gourd onto a bow. A tin can or plastic container with one end removed may also be used. Attach it to the bow with a wire or small screw.

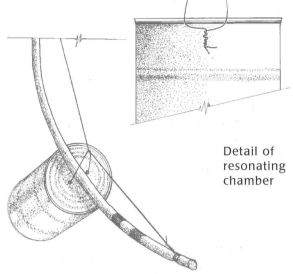

Detail of resonating chamber

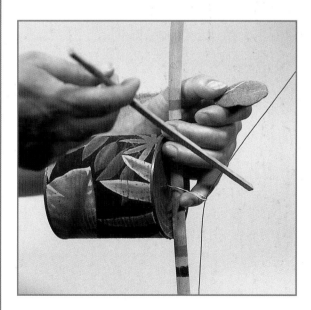

Berimbau

In Brazil, the berimbau, a two-note bow, accompanies a martial arts dance, called capoeira. The gourd is held to the bow by a noose, dividing the string into two vibrating sections of different pitch. A flat rock or large coin held in the left hand adds an additional note by pressing it against the string while the right hand strikes the string with a stick.

DIDDLY BOW

The American diddly bow probably originated in poor rural areas of the South where it was made from whatever material was at hand. Traditionally, a stout wire was secured between two nails hammered into the wall of a house or barn, then tensioned by one or more bridges jammed under the string. The string was then strummed while sliding a hard object along it. The following instrument project is a portable and tunable adaptation of the diddly bow.

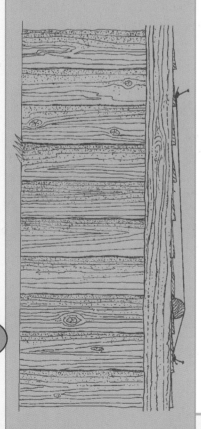

Materials
1 in x 2 in board, 2 to 3 ft long
Small wood scraps for 2 bridges
Tuning mechanism and stout nail for securing string
Length of strong wire
Bottleneck or steel slide guitar noter
Guitar pick

Tools
Saw
Hammer
Drill
Sandpaper

Assembly
1 Sand board smooth.
2 Prepare one end for tuning mechanism.
3 Hammer nail into other end.
4 Glue both bridges onto board.
5 Secure string and tighten.
6 Prepare a bottleneck and pick and start strumming.

To Play
The portable diddly bow sounds best when placed on a resonating surface (desk or tabletop). Use bottleneck from wine bottle or 3 in segment of 1-in-diameter metal electrical pipe for noter. Slide up and down string as you strum.

WASHTUB BASS

This folk instrument is common to jug bands, skiffle bands, and other "down home" musical groups. It resembles the African ground bow and gives a strong rhythmic pulse.

Materials
Metal washtub
3 or 4 ft nylon cord
¾ in diameter wood doweling or broomstick, 4 to 5 ft long
Screw eye, 2 washers and nuts

Tools
Saw
Hammer
Drill with ¼ in bit

Assembly
1 Drill a hole 1 in from end of stick.
2 Saw a groove in other end perpendicular to direction of hole. This groove will notch on rim of tub (different styles of tubs might require different treatments).
3 Punch hole in center of bottom part of tub.
4 Thread screw eye through hole and secure with washers and nuts.
5 Thread string through screw-eye hole.
6 Thread free end of string through hole in stick and tie securely.

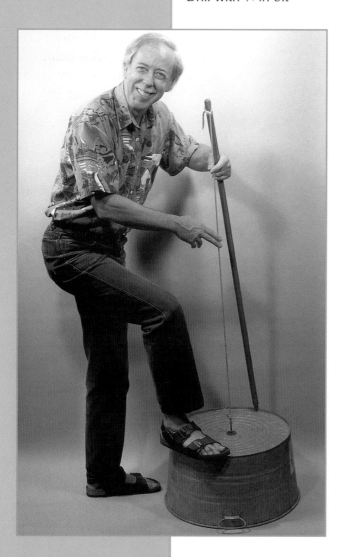

To Play
1 Hook notched end of stick over edge or onto raised rim of tub bottom.
2 Brace tub by putting one foot on opposite side of rim.
3 Tighten or loosen tension of string by gently pulling stick backward and forward with your left hand causing pitch to change. Pulling the stick back tightens the string, making it sound higher.
4 Pluck string with your right hand and slowly pull back on stick to discover its range. Then loosen string until it ceases to make a clear sound.
5 Place a book-size piece of wood under one edge of tub to hold it away from floor.

The pitch of the washtub bass need not be exact to get the desired effect. It can lay down an accurate bass line, but its most important factor is the low rhythmic effect. Some players pluck and strum using a glove to protect the fingers.

Ground Bow or Pit Harp

A variation of the washtub bass is the ground bow or pit harp (Africa) or mosquito drum (Haiti). The earth as resonator gives a deep mellow tone.

Make your own by digging a small pit in the earth about one foot deep. Secure a pole in ground and bend the end over the pit. Cover the pit with rubber, leather skins, a sheet of metal, thick cardboard, or a thin sheet of plywood and secure with stones, stakes, or tent pegs. Punch a hole in center of cover. Tie 4 to 5 ft of twine, nylon string, or wire to a small stick or nail and thread line through this hole. Tie from membrane to stick end.

To play, steady and flex end of stick with one hand and pluck or strum string with the other hand. Subtle pitches are produced by increasing and decreasing the tension of the string. A second player can play directly on the skin-covering with drum sticks.

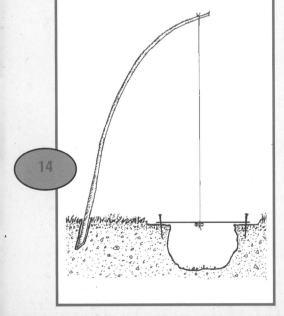

EKTAR

This folk instrument is commonly used in India and neighboring countries to accompany singing and storytelling. Its clever string arrangement and resulting portamento sliding effect are unique features. Gourds, split bamboo, and animal hide are traditional construction materials.

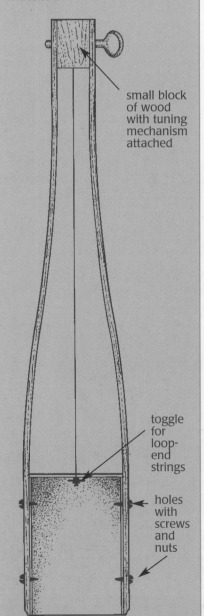

small block of wood with tuning mechanism attached

toggle for loop-end strings

holes with screws and nuts

Materials
2 lengths of garden lattice, or yardsticks, or strips of ⅛ in plywood, 2 to 3 ft long
Medium-size tin can container
Short screws and nuts
Tuning mechanism
Thin string (.010 in diameter)

Tools
Saw
Drill and bit
Screwdriver
Glue
Sandpaper

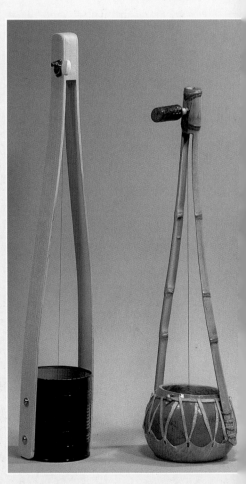

Assembly

1 Drill two holes in each strip of wood and can, as shown.

2 Attach them to opposite sides of tin can and secure them with screws and nuts.

3 Connect other ends of wood strips with a small block of wood drilled to accommodate an appropriate tuning mechanism (see diagram below for mounting tuner).

4 Punch small hole in center of metal end of tin can or plastic lid that replaces the tin. The metal end will produce a brighter sound.

5 Pass string through hole and secure to tuner. Make a small toggle for loop-end strings so string will not pull through the end of the can.

6 Tighten string to a low tension.

To Play

Hold the instrument, as shown, and strum the string rhythmically while squeezing the wood strips. The pitch should rise and fall as you flex the wood. Squeezing at different points along the wood lengths will produce a variety of effects.

Detail of tuning mechanism

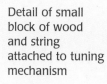

Detail of small block of wood and string attached to tuning mechanism

15

BLEACH BOTTLE BANJO

The basic idea for the banjo probably developed in Africa hundreds of years ago and transferred to the Americas during the slave trade era when simply fashioned stringed instruments were made by rural folk using whatever was at hand. This bleach bottle banjo belongs to the lute family of instruments that includes the guitar, bluegrass banjo, mandolin, and all other stringed instruments with a neck. I call this do-it-yourself project a banjo, but its design and construction are based on the traditional practice of spiking a length of wood through a sound box resonator made from materials such as a calabash, coconut shell, cigar box, or a plastic container.

Materials
2 to 4 qt size plastic container
30 in x 1 in x 2 in wood strip for the neck
3 yds nylon fishing line (40 to 60 lb test)
¾ in x 2 in x ¼ in piece of wood for bridge
2 screw eyes or other tuner options
2—1 in finishing nails for hitch pins

Tools
Saw
Hammer
Utility knife
Sandpaper

Assembly
1   Cut off bottom half of plastic container. On opposite sides of container, cut trap door flaps close to the resonator playing surface so that the fingerboard fits snugly when the flaps of the container are folded out and the wood strip is inserted (see photo).

2   At the tail of the instrument, hammer in hitch pins side by side so that only a small portion of the nail protrudes. At the head of the instrument, place screw eyes so when turned they do not bump into each other. Do not screw them in too far until after strings are attached.

3   Secure fishing line strings between nails and screws. Tie knots so they will not slip when tensioning strings.

4   Insert small chunk of wood under strings for bridge. Cut shallow slots into bridge to keep strings from sliding off.

5   Add a small piece of wood next to the screw eyes (tuning pegs) for nut. See Making Frets, p17.

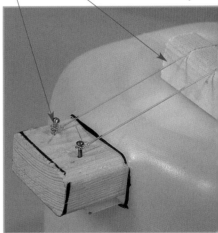

hitch pins   bridge   tail end of banjo

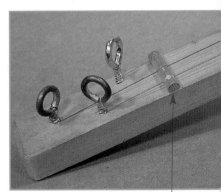

head of 3-string banjo   nut

6 Tension strings by turning screw eyes into wood. Make adjustments where necessary. Strings should be fairly tight for maximum resonance.

7 Paint or decorate resonator, if desired.

To Play

Tune the strings to create whatever pitch relationship you wish. I suggest unison tuning: one string acts as a drone, the other as a melody string. After tuning, hold and strum the instrument in guitar-like fashion. By stopping the melody string along the board neck with your fingers, you can pick out scales and melodies. Making fret marks with a felt-tip pen at appropriate places along the fingerboard will help you find the scale notes. I prefer a regular do-re-mi diatonic (rather than chromatic) scale for playing simple melodies.

Making Frets

Add a small piece of wood (a nut) next to the tuning pegs to delineate a more precise string length between nut and bridge. Notes of a major scale can be marked on the fingerboard or make simple frets using ¾ in dowels flattened on one side and glued along the fingerboard at the appropriate places. See the stick dulcimer, p18, for other fret alternatives. The nut should be notched and should raise the strings just enough above the fingerboard to pass slightly above the first fret. If the strings bump into frets farther along the fingerboard while fingering the first three or four frets, raise the height of the bridge slightly to correct this.

nut   frets

17

STICK DULCIMER

This simplified version of the Appalachian dulcimer is sometimes humorously called a "dulciless" because of its abbreviated design. Derived from various historical European folk zithers, the Appalachian version evolved in the southeastern mountain ranges of North America and is one of the very few truly American folk instruments.

Materials

30 in x 1 in x 2 in wood stick
Medium-size screw eyes or other tuning peg option
¼ in dowel (sanded flat on one side) for bridge and nut
2–1st or 2nd guitar strings
2–1 in nails for hitch pins

Tools

Hammer
Screwdriver
Staple gun and staples for frets
Wood glue

Assembly

1 Draw lines on the board for the nut, bridge, and fret/staples, as shown.

2 Insert the staples as carefully as possible. If the staples don't go in far enough, just tap them gently with a hammer. If they go in too far, pry them up slightly with a screwdriver. They should stand up ¹⁄₁₆ in above the surface of the fingerboard.

3 Flatten one side of each dowel and glue to the board, as shown, making sure there is exactly 27 in between their centers.

4 Install screw eyes or pegs at one end and nails at other end, as shown. Line everything up carefully so that the melody string passes over the frets.

5 Loop string onto nail and tie securely, then wrap other end around screw eye so that it will tension as you screw the mechanism into the wood.

6 Tune by turning the screw until the string sounds pleasant and is comfortably tight. Use a dowel or nail for leverage.

7 Make small notches in the nut and bridge to keep the string from slipping around and to set the action. At the nut the string should be about ⅛ in above the fingerboard and at the bridge ⅜ in.

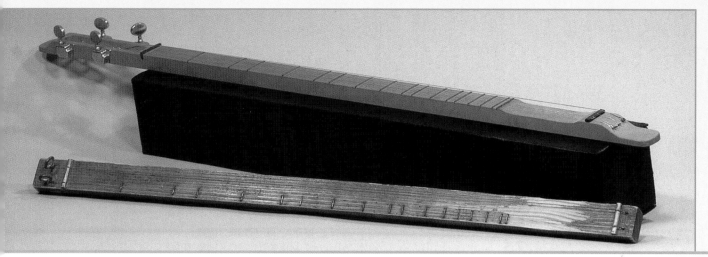

To Play

The scale (frets) on dulcimers is always laid out in a diatonic pattern equivalent to a white key scale on the piano. (do-re-mi-fa-sol-la-ti-do arrangement). Making a melody or noting is usually done with a finger or a dowel (4 to 5 in long by ¼ in diameter) held firmly in the left hand. This noter helps slide from note to note. The right hand strums an appropriate rhythm with a fair size guitar pick or plectrum made from a plastic bottle. Traditionally, a goose or turkey quill shaved flat on the end was used for strumming. Tune the two strings in unison (both sounding the same pitch). Make a major scale by simply noting up the melody string. The dulcimer is a modal based instrument and can achieve other tonalities as well. To access other modes, it is best to buy a dulcimer book that has all the tuning explanations. Place the stick on a desk top or a cardboard box, to increase the volume. For instructions on making more complicated dulcimers with sound boxes, see p84.

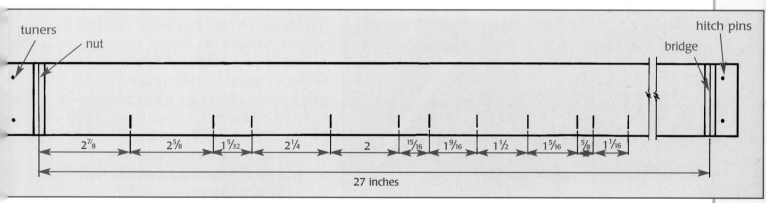

tuners

nut

hitch pins

bridge

| 2⁷/₈ | 2⁵/₈ | 1⁵/₃₂ | 2¼ | 2 | ¹⁵/₁₆ | 1⁹/₁₆ | 1½ | 1⁵/₁₆ | ⁵/₈ | 1¹/₁₆ |

27 inches

SHOE BOX ZITHER

This rubber band shoe box zither reveals much information about the underlying principle of all stringed instruments. Connecting a vibrating body (the strings) to a resonating chamber (a sound box) reinforces the vibratory surface thus enhancing the quality of the sound and making it louder. This basic relationship between vibrating string and a container of enclosed air satisfies two of the most important factors involved in making stringed instruments.

Materials

Several sizes of rubber bands (thin, fat, short, long)
Sturdy containers (match boxes, shoe boxes, cigar boxes, plastic cups or glasses, wide-mouth tin cans)
2 pencils or dowels for bridges

Tools

Utility knife

Assembly

1 Remove lid and place rubber bands around container so they stretch over opening. If they are too loose or too tight, make adjustments with larger or smaller bands. You may need to reinforce your sound box with braces or struts to keep it from collapsing under the tension of the rubber bands. Pluck each band and adjust until it responds with a reasonable pitch.

2 A clearer sound may be achieved by placing pencils or dowels under the rubber bands at each end of the box. The pencils act as simple bridges to delineate an exact string length and a more precise pitch. You might also experiment by placing only one pencil under the rubber bands at the center of the box and plucking on either side. Move the pencil slightly to one side for an increased range of high and low notes.

3 Option   Cut a hole in the center of the box lid and place it back on the box. Add rubber bands and put the pencil bridges back under the rubber bands towards the ends of the box. The top acts as a simple soundboard and will change the sound characteristics of the box appreciably. By slightly stretching or loosening the rubber bands between the bridges, you can create a simple scale or even compose a short musical piece.

BOARD ZITHER

Zithers make up one of the most ancient of all instrument families. Unlike chordophones in the lute family, zithers have sound boxes with no neck and can have any number of strings that stretch from one end of the sound box to the other. Typical members of this family include Renaissance psaltery, Austrian zither, folk autoharp, and Japanese koto. In some ways, the harpsichord and piano manifest highly developed forms of this ancient family. Though most zithers are plucked, many, such as the piano, are tapped with hammers or mallets (see hammered dulcimer, p84). The electric steel guitar, a fairly recent invention popular in Hawaiian and country music, is also a zither, sometimes boasting multiple fingerboards, knee levers, and foot pedals.

Materials

¾ in x 6 to 8 in wide pine or plywood board, 8 to 10 in long
Nylon fishing line or metal guitar strings
1 in nails with heads
Screw eyes

Tools

Hammer
Ruler
Awl or large nail
Saw
Sandpaper

Assembly

1 Draw a line with a ruler about 1 in from end and parallel to the end of the board.

2 Draw another line slanting from slightly over halfway up the side towards the opposite corner.

3 Hammer a row of nails at ½ in intervals partway into the board along the parallel line. Any number of strings is acceptable. Try starting with just four or five and expand later to a full octave.

4 Using an awl or large nail to start the holes, insert screw eyes partway into the board along the other line opposite the nails.

5 Attach the fishing line or guitar string firmly to a nail then pull the string tight and wrap and tie securely around each screw eye. Tighten the strings by turning the screw eyes. Use a nail inserted through the screw eye as leverage for tuning.

6 Tune the strings to a scale with the help of a piano or pitch pipe. The strings will sound best if they are reasonably taut.

7 You can paint, stencil, or wood burn designs on the face of the board or drill a sound hole under the strings.

To Play

The strings may be tuned to any scale, but a diatonic scale (do-re-mi-fa-sol-la-ti-do arrangement) is most useful. Make sure that you are aware of how tight the strings are as you tune up. Otherwise there is some risk of breaking them. Be ready to adjust to a lower scale if they seem too tight or to a higher scale if they seem too loose. Hold the zither next to your ear or place it on a resonating surface and pluck the strings with your fingers or a guitar pick. If your instrument has an appropriate range, you should be able to pick out familiar simple melodies. A sound box may be attached to the board for more resonance but in this case you should use a thinner piece of wood for the top. A design for a more sophisticated zither (psaltery) is described on p22.

PSALTERY

The psaltery is a branch of the zither family of chordophones and is thus characterized by multiple strings on a sound box with no neck. The style of psaltery suggested here is an extension of the previous two instruments in this section: the shoe box zither and the board zither. European styles of the psaltery are seen in many Medieval and Renaissance paintings and they enjoyed widespread popularity until psalteries with keyboards such as the clavichord and harpsichord took precedence.

Materials
⅛ in plywood, 13 in x 12 in for top and back
12 in x 1 in x 1 in stick of maple or other hardwood for end blocks
20 in x 1 in x ½ in stick of maple for sides
7 in x ½ in x ⅜ in strip of maple or other hardwood for bridges
8 zither pins and 8 hitch pins or ¾ in finishing nails
7 in length of 3/32 in steel rod or coat hanger
.014 in and .016 in music wire (guitar or banjo strings)

Tools
Wood glue
Saws (jigsaw, coping, or fret saw)
Drill and bits to match zither pins and hitch pins
Clamps, weights, and/or strong rubber bands
Plane
Sandpaper and finishing materials
Zither pin tuning wrench (type used for autoharps)

Assembly

1 Cut plywood into two equal pieces for top (soundboard) and bottom (back) of psaltery.

2 On top piece draw a 1¼ in diameter circle, as shown. Drill it out with a circle cutter using a drill press, or drill a small hole and use a coping saw, fret saw, or jigsaw to cut around penciled area.

3 From the 12 in x 1 in x 1 in stick, cut two pieces for end blocks.

4 Glue and clamp end blocks to back. Let dry.

5 From the 20 in x 1 in x ½ in hardwood stick, cut side pieces so they fit between the end blocks, along sides of instrument. Measure carefully for a good fit. Glue into place.

6 You may have to plane or sand the sides and end blocks first to insure good contact with the top. Check carefully before applying glue. Glue on top. Hold until dry with clamps, weights, or rubber bands.

7 Position the 7 in x ½ in x ⅜ in strip onto the soundboard, as shown. Option   A length of steel rod or coat hanger may be placed in a groove on top of the bridge to keep the strings from cutting into the wood. The groove can be incised by hand or cut with a small hand router (a Dremel tool).

8 Glue the bridge in place. Clamp and let dry.

9 Drill holes to receive zither pins. Test on a scrap piece of wood to make sure the drilled hole will hold the pins firmly. Drill holes at a slight angle.

10 Drill holes to receive hitch pins. Piano bridge pins are good for this purpose or use ¾ in finishing nails. Pre-drill holes to prevent wood from splitting.

11 Sand sound box. Stain or decorate with paint. Apply finishing materials, see p117.

12 Hammer or screw in zither pins leaving enough protruding for a few more twists as strings are attached. Use a tuning wrench made for zither pins.

13 Gently hammer in hitch pins.

14 String by tying a loop in the end of each string, as shown.

15 Place steel rod in bridge groove.

16 Tune to desired scale. Strings should be relatively tight for a bell-like sound. Several tunings may be necessary before the strings settle in and stabilize. Tune to a piano or have a musician help you with the initial tuning.

To Play

Play as suggested for the board zither (p21). Simple chords and two- and three-note harmonies sound harp-like and quite beautiful.

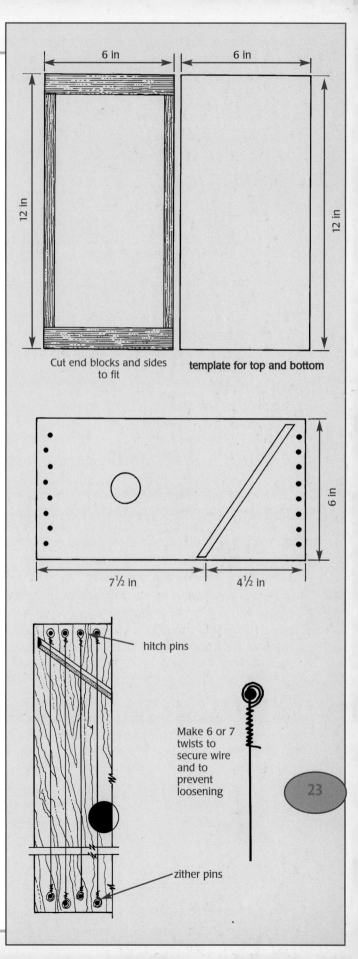

6 in   6 in

12 in

Cut end blocks and sides to fit

12 in

template for top and bottom

6 in

7½ in   4½ in

hitch pins

Make 6 or 7 twists to secure wire and to prevent loosening

zither pins

23

SIMPLE FOLK INSTRUMENTS

Aerophones

The infinite diversity of wind instruments in the aerophone family is as rich as that of the stringed chordophone family. Their use dates back to prehistoric times as evidenced by the remains of bone flutes and conch shell horns unearthed by archeologists. Through the centuries, wind instruments have accompanied triumphant marching from Roman conquerors to Aztec ceremonial gatherings. The mythical Pied Piper used a wind instrument to cast spells of enchantment over animals and humans and the devastating powerful horns of Gabriel heralded the final Judgment Day. In contemporary times, brass and other wind instruments such as the Scottish bagpipes lead armies to war, inspire nationalistic fervor, and add pomp and splendor to festive occasions. But wind instruments are also used in more meditative and philosophical circumstances. Some American Indians use particular flutes to play delicate songs to court their women and East Indian musicians use the bamboo flute to produce subtly embellished mystical music as an important part of religious expression.

Aerophones vibrate a column of air and are thus acoustically more difficult to understand than stringed instruments but basically a longer column of air means lower pitch; short equals high. Wind instruments also require specialized techniques for blowing.

There are three categories of wind instruments: flutes, reeds, and horns. Flutes (and whistles) include those instruments with a small blow hole towards one end and a series of fingerholes arranged in various spacings and patterns down the length of the instrument. With end-blown flutes such as the Irish penny whistle and recorder, the air is blown through a mouthpiece that automatically forces the air to split over a sharp edge to produce the sound. Transverse (side-blown) flutes require the player to form an embouchure, forming the lips in such a way to focus air at the tone-producing edge. The modern silver flute found in orchestras shows a highly developed mechanical design with its many keys and levers. Around the world flutes are constructed according to local ecology: wood, bamboo, clay, stone, and bone from animals and even humans. Most flutes, however, are made of bamboo and are keyless.

Reed instruments utilize thin flexible reeds activated by air for tone production. Children use the reed principle when they blow through a blade of grass between their thumbs or blow the squeezed end of a soda straw to produce a squawk. The highly sophisticated oboe and English horn work on the same double reed principle as the soda straw. An unusual variation includes the Scottish bagpipes where air is blown into a leather bag and then squeezed through a series of pipes that have reeds inside. This arrangement gives a constant uninterrupted sound. Clarinets and saxophones use only a single reed on specially fashioned mouthpieces for sound production.

In contrast, trumpet and other horn players vibrate or buzz their lips into a cup-shaped mouthpiece to sound their instruments. Tightening and loosening lips raises and lowers the pitch respectively. Early horns such as the ram's horn and the conch shell trumpet depended on a phenomenon called the overtone series for making different pitches. Later, holes were added to achieve greater variety. Eventually modern construction techniques added valves, slides, and tubing to facilitate melodic movement between notes.

BASIC WINDS

Simple wind instruments rely on a column of vibrating air to produce sound. The following projects are easy to make and provide opportunities to experiment with sound production.

Pen Cap Panpipes
Collect all the larger, longer ballpoint and felt-tip pen caps you can find. Blow strongly across the open end of each cap. Different sizes produce various pitches. If you have difficulty making them speak, change the angle of blowing slightly. (Some pen caps may be too small to give a clear pitch.) Arrange them high to low and tape them together to make a set of simple panpipes.

Straw Oboe
Find some waxed paper straws (easier to play) or plastic straws. Flatten about ½ in of one end of the paper straw and snip off a little of the corners with scissors. If you use plastic straws, flatten about 1 in and carefully make a short quarter-inch slit down the crease with a knife. Snip the corners.

Put the cut end into your mouth just past your lips and blow. Adjust the pressure of your lips and move the straw a little farther into or out of your mouth until you get a good squawk. Try poking a finger hole or two into the straw towards the end opposite your mouth and see if you can produce a simple scale. Cut other straws to different lengths and have your friends squawk along in harmony.

Blade-of-Grass Squawker
Place a blade of grass or a thin strip of resilient paper between the edges of your thumbs (the blade is held snugly between the two knuckles) so a blow hole is created between them. Hold it to your mouth so you can blow through the passage onto the edge of the paper or grass blade. Blow fairly hard and make adjustments until you can produce a good loud squawk or screech. Replace grass or paper after a few blows.

Comb and Tissue Kazoo
Though not truly a wind instrument, the kazoo fits this section because it uses the mouth and voice for its effect. Find a comb with big teeth not too close together and fold a piece of tissue paper or wax paper (thin, lightweight but firm) over the comb teeth. Place the flat side of the comb to your lips and hum vigorously through the paper. The buzzing quality will add a new and fun dimension to your songs.

Bottle Calliope

Blow across the tops of various pop bottles, water bottles, wine bottles, beer bottles, and other bottles with small openings. Every bottle has a definite pitch, depending on its size. More specifically, the pitch is determined by each bottle's inner volume of air. By adding certain amounts of water, you can raise or lower the pitch. Adding water makes the volume of air in the bottle smaller and thus raises the pitch produced. In fact, you can actually create a scale using a row of similarly-sized bottles with carefully graduated volumes of water. Now you can play real melodies. Organize a bottle band by having your friends blow different rhythms on different size bottles.

Musical Jugs

The traditional jug band got its name from the musical jug, an instrument—usually a whisky jug—that produces a tuba-like rhythmic bass line. Almost any bottle or jug produces a deep pitch when air is blown across the spout opening. However, buzzing the lips loosely as you blow creates a new quality of sound more common to the musical stylings of jug bands. Better players actually produce different pitches by tightening and loosening the lips as one would on a tuba or trombone.

Bull Roarer

Though not a wind instrument in the traditional sense (you don't blow it), the bull roarer makes the air vibrate and thus is considered an aerophone. To make, tie 3 to 6 ft of strong string or twine through a hole drilled in one end of a flat piece of wood 12 in by 2 in by $\frac{3}{8}$ in thick. Make sure the string knot is well secured.

Swing the bull roarer overhead until it begins to spin in the air causing a whirring sound. If you have trouble getting the wood to rotate, try winding up the string a little before swinging. The speed of the swing and the size of the wood control the quality of the roar.

FLUTES

Archeologists list flutes as one of man's earliest pieces of technology dating back to Neanderthal times, 43,000 to 82,000 years ago! It has remained one of the most universal of all instrument types, utilizing the principle of a stream of air that splits over a sharp edge causing a vibrational wave that we perceive as sound.

PANPIPES

Panpipes have sometimes been called Pan's flute after the Greek god of forests, pastures, and shepherds. They are commonly fashioned from bamboo—but can also be made from wood, clay, and synthetic materials such as PVC, ABS, or other high-tech plastic tubing. Panpipes are particularly outstanding in the folk music of Hungary, Peru, and Africa.

Materials
⅜ to 1 in diameter stiff plastic tubing, 5 ft long
Plugs for tube ends (rubber stoppers, corks, or plasticine clay)
Tape, string, or appropriate glue to hold pipes together

Tools
Saw
Ruler
Sandpaper

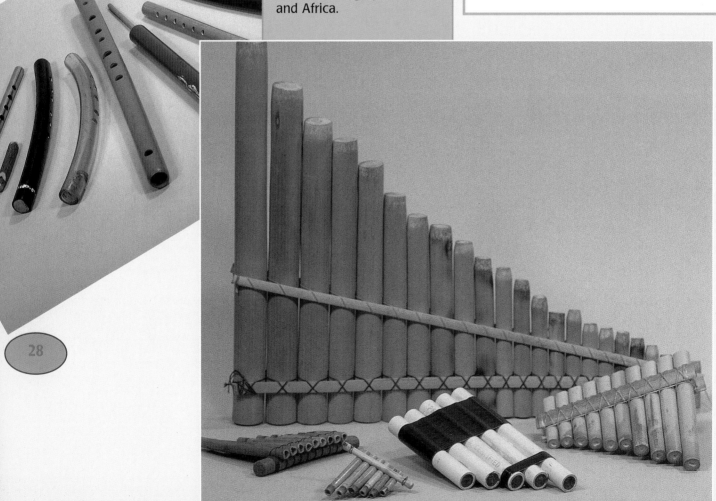

Assembly

1 Use any number of pipes you wish. Remember, the longer the pipe, the lower the pitch. Adjust pitch by trimming off length or pushing stoppers farther into the tube.

2 If you prefer, cut a set of tubes that make a specific scale. You may do this by ear or use the following measurements as a general guide. These lengths should approximate a G major scale if a ⅝ in diameter tubing is used. Make adjustments as necessary.

do	8⅜ in	sol	5⅜ in
re	7½ in	la	4¾ in
mi	6½ in	ti	4¼ in
fa	6 in	do	4 in

3 Organize pipes as a scale and glue or tape together for stability. A decorative strip of cloth can be glued around the pipes to help secure them. Sticks may also be laced on either side of the tubes for a decorative effect.

To Play

Use the same blowing technique as blowing across the top of a bottle (see bottle calliope, p27). Practice moving the pipes accurately across your lips. South Americans play them with great facility and speed. It takes a lot of wind to play the pipes so take a deep breath as often as necessary. You might also hand out single pipes to a group of people and play them in the fashion of a hand-bell ensemble. Each person is responsible for a pitch or two within the context of a song. Playing at the right moment in coordination with the others forms a coherent melody.

Using bamboo

If you live in an area where bamboo grows, try making a flute with it. You may have to open up the bamboo tube by drilling through the natural nodal partitions of the wood to get the proper lengths. Alternatively, you can use the nodes as the stopped end on the panpipes and trim from the other end to reach the desired pitch. The skin of the bamboo will splinter unless great care is taken. Traditionally, blow holes and fingerholes were burned (instead of drilled) into the bamboo with a very hot poker. Whether you burn or drill, do not inhale bamboo dust or smoke.

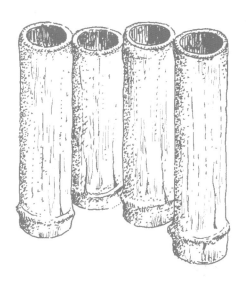

PIPE RECORDER

This branch of the flute family uses a gentle end-blowing technique to produce the tone. The mouthpiece design (a fipple) does not require the player to form the lips in a precise way. During Medieval and Renaissance periods in Europe, different sizes of flutes of this type called recorders were combined into families or consorts to make music.

Materials
¾ in diameter stiff plastic tube, 12 in long (Polypipe, PVC, ABS, or bamboo)
Cork or wood dowel (same diameter as inside of tube)

Tools
Sharp knife (saw or file for bamboo)
³⁄₁₆ to ¼ in drill bit and drill
Sandpaper
Small round file
Small saw

Assembly

1 If using bamboo, carefully clear out joints with drill or sharp tool.

2 Measure 1 in from end and cut sound-producing opening, as shown. Note   Opening must be as clean and precise as possible. Use knife, file, and saw.

3 Select a short piece of doweling or wine cork that fits snugly into the tube. Sand or cut one side by placing sandpaper flat on table and working piece to correct shape. Make sure sanded area is at a slight incline like a ramp, and flat and smooth so air will project across opening and hit edge, as shown.

4 Place plug into end of pipe so slanted surface inclines towards the sound-producing opening. Insert plug so that it is flush with the opening.

5 Position plug so that the air from your mouth will rush through the narrow channel, cross the opening, and split over the sharp edge at the other side of the hole.

6 Blowing softly should produce a clear note. If recorder doesn't play well at first, move plug backward or forward in small adjustments. If you feel

too much resistance when you blow, try sanding off the slanted portion of the plug a little bit at a time. If it blows easy enough but with no response, try sanding the slant a little steeper. If you sand too much off the plug, start again with another dowel or cork.

Finger Hole Placement

Experimenting with hole placement can be a very creative experience. Many cultures in the world create their own unique tonal systems based on their historical and aesthetic sensibilities. Scales can have any number of notes so flute makers must experiment by using various configurations and numbers of finger holes. In this spirit, you might consider creating your own unique scale as an individual musical trademark.

1 If you choose a standard tuned scale for your recorder, tune the pipe to a fundamental pitch by cutting off a little at a time from the end opposite the mouthpiece.

2 Draw a straight line the length of the pipe from the center of the mouthpiece opening to the opposite end.

3 Using the ¼ in bit, drill first hole 1½ to 2 in from the open end opposite the mouthpiece.

4 For fine tuning, you can make the note a little higher by enlarging it. If hole becomes too enlarged, add a bit of tape over part of the hole to correct it.

5 Drill each hole one at a time using the approximate measurements shown.

6 You can drill an optional thumb hole opposite the uppermost hole on the other side for an extra note.

To Play

1 Try blowing very soft while moving your fingers in sequence from low to high. Hard blowing is not usually advisable, but *may* produce an upper register of notes.

2 Try half-holing or sliding your fingers slowly off the finger holes.

3 Try different combinations of fingers for new pitches or compose a tune.

4 If you have made a recorder tuned to a standard scale, begin by covering all the holes (making sure the holes are completely covered) and blow softly. Lift one finger at a time starting at the end opposite of the mouthpiece until all the holes are open. Then, if you're lucky, by covering all the holes again and blowing harder you may be able to play a higher-pitched scale using the same procedure.

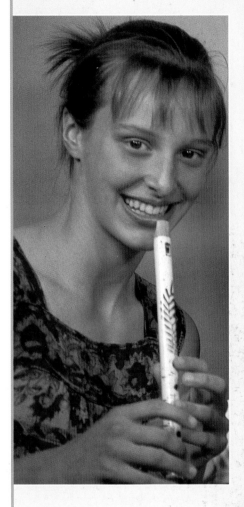

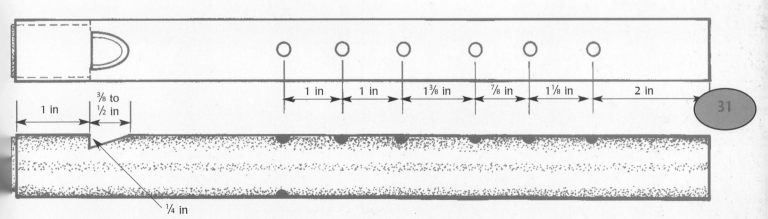

Twig Whistle

The twig whistle works on the same principle as the pipe recorder. A twig chosen from a dead or dry branch is best so it won't shrink or crack over time.

Materials
Dried twig 4 to 5 in long, ½ in or more in diameter
Wood doweling same size as drill bit

Tools
Drill with an appropriate drill bit
Small saw

Assembly

1 Drill out center of twig stopping short of drilling through the full length.

2 Carefully cut a small notch, as shown, about ½ in from blowing end.

3 Sand about ⅓ in of the doweling flat (see pipe recorder instructions, p30).

4 Insert dowel into twig and adjust until a whistle is produced.

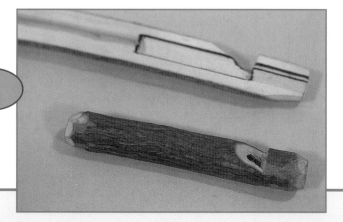

OCARINA

Earthenware ocarinas (terra cotta vessel flutes) date back as early as 1766 B.C. in China. In later Mayan and Aztec civilizations, ocarinas were made in a variety of zoomorphic and anthropomorphic shapes and sizes. In Europe, the ocarina was called a "sweet potato" because of its characteristic shape. The sound-producing principle of the ocarina is identical to the hose pipe recorder although the difference in materials requires a different process.

Materials
Polymer clay (such as Fimo® or Sculpey®) that is baked in a standard oven, or low-fire clay, if a kiln is available

Tools
Selection of little sticks, splints, and pokers for making flute window and windway

Assembly

1 Begin with palm-size lump of clay and pinch it into roundish cup shape leaving rim of cup relatively thick.

2 Pull the rim over the opening forming it into a beak shape, as shown.

3 Make a window into the vessel with a small flat splint.

4 With the same implement create a windway through the beak and through the plane of the window.

5 On the side of the window opposite the windway, use a splint to press the clay into a wedge so that the air will pass through the windway, across the window, and split on the edge of the wedge. (See instructions for pipe recorder, p30.)

6 In making adjustments to get a first sound, breathe gently into the instrument. This will get quicker results than blowing hard. After getting a sound, poke finger holes, as shown. Make three or four holes. If sound is not good, smooth over hole and try another location.

7 Decorate and bake or fire, depending on materials used.

Making cup shape with thick rim

Creating the beak shape

Making windway into vessel

Measuring for position of window

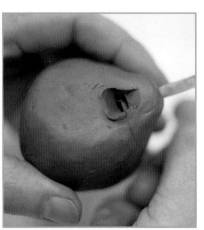

Making wedge so air will pass through windway, across window, and split on edge of wedge

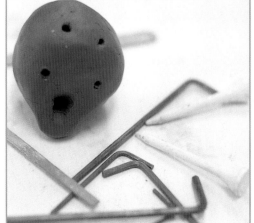

Making finger holes

33

SLIDE WHISTLE

The slide whistle is constructed much like the recorder with the exception that the pitch is changed by varying the length of the tube with a plunger instead of with finger holes.

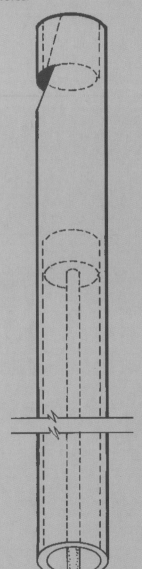

Materials
1 ft firm plastic tubing or any thin-walled plastic pipe, bamboo, wood tube, or thin-walled metal tubing
Piece of doweling or cork to fit inside diameter of tube for the mouthpiece
Length of small diameter doweling a bit longer than the tube to be used for the slider
Small scrap of plastic sponge or a cork about ½ in thick for plunger
Glue

Tools
Sharp knife
Sandpaper
File
Saw

Assembly
1 Cut sponge plunger slightly larger than the inside diameter of tube or sand cork to fit in tube.
2 Glue sponge or cork to end of dowel slide.
3 Fit the slide snugly inside tube and adjust to slide smoothly.
4 Carefully cut sound-producing window with knife, file, or saw. Shape dowel or cork fipple and test the mouthpiece. Experiment and make adjustments until you can produce a strong steady tone. Refer to p30 for details.

To Play
The slide whistle has always been a favorite because of its special sliding or portamento quality. It is not often used in serious music, but can be heard often in cartoons.

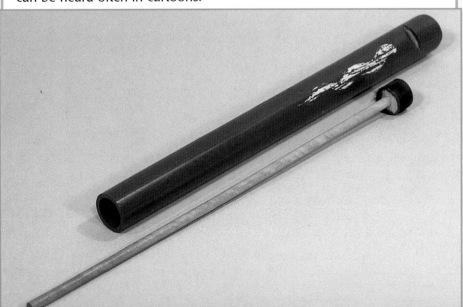

Transverse flutes are held across the face and blown through a hole on the side of the tube instead of the end. They are known in every culture and can be made from stone, metal, wood, clay, ceramic, bone, bamboo, and reed. The lips must be formed in a particular fashion to make the sound.

Materials
¾ in diameter plumber's PVC or ABS pipe, 1 to 1½ ft long
Short segment of cork or other material that will snugly fit into end of pipe

Tools
Saw or tube-cutter
Drill and ¼ in or ⁵⁄₁₆ in bit
Round file

Assembly

1 Cut pipe to 17³⁄₁₆ in length.

2 Place cork in end of pipe. Shape for a tight seal.

3 Drill blow hole about 1 in from closed end. Refine hole by filing to an oval shape about ⅜ in across. Give it a slightly chamfered (beveled) edge and adjust size and shape to produce a strong sustained sound.

4 Experiment with how far the cork should fit into the end of the tube.

5 Make a scale by using the measurements shown below, OR create your own scale by placing fingerholes along the flute by drilling a ¼ in hole, 2 in from the end opposite the mouthpiece and test it. Drill another hole about 1 in higher than the first and experiment with that. Add more holes 1 in apart. Do not drill holes within 4 in of blow hole. Drill thumb hole opposite the uppermost fingerhole.

To Play
Hold flute, as shown. Blow gently and obliquely *across* blow hole. Place flute to your mouth so that a thin stream of air is projected from your lips to the opposite side of the hole. Practice makes a sustained sound.

⅜ in

1 in

1 in	7¼ in	1⁵⁄₁₆ in	1⅜ in	1⅝ in	1 in	1⅝ in	2 in

17³⁄₁₆ in

HORNS AND TRUMPETS

Natural animal horn trumpets and conch shell trumpets have been used throughout history as signaling devices because of their volume and great audible range. Horns have been used for hunting, to coordinate troop movements in battle, to send messages, to signal the arrival of strangers, or to contact the spirit world.

HOSE BUGLE

In the 18th century, brass instruments had no valves and players used their lips to make different notes. With long lengths of tubing the player can produce a wide spectrum of pitches using natural overtones called the harmonic series.

Materials
Hose or synthetic tubing, 3 to 10 ft long
Trumpet or other brass instrument mouthpiece
Funnel (plastic or metal)
Tape

Assembly

1 If you use garden hose, decide whether or not to leave the metal connectors on or to remove them. The male metal connector could be used for the mouthpiece or secure an instrument mouthpiece to the end of the hose if connector is removed.

2 Secure funnel on other end by jamming it into the end of the hose. If necessary, wrap tape around the narrow part of the funnel before inserting or place the funnel into the hose and wrap tape around the point where they connect.

To Play
Buzz your lips into the mouthpiece and try changing the pitch by tightening and loosening your lip pressure slightly. You can play the instrument as a bugle or simply make elephant-like sounds. If you find it difficult to make a sound, ask a brass instrument player to give you a demonstration.

COW HORN TRUMPET

This primitive instrument makes a good, strong sound.

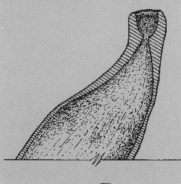

Materials
Cow horn or other animal horn
Trumpet, bugle, or cornet
  mouthpiece

Tools
Saw
Knife
Drill and bit (bit size is
  determined by shank size of
  mouthpiece)

Assembly

1 Purchase a horn from a craft store, taxidermist, veterinarian, or slaughterhouse. A fresh animal horn must be processed as follows:
  a) Boil horn 2 hours or until marrow becomes soft.
  b) Scrape and carve out all marrow from inside.
  c) Sand and polish horn until smooth and shiny.

2 Cut off pointed end of horn a little at a time until shank of your chosen mouthpiece fits snugly into the hole. Alternatively, cut off the tip of the horn and drill a hole into the end so the mouth piece will fit. Or, if horn is large and thick, a cup-shaped recess may be carved directly into the end of the horn, thus bypassing the need of a trumpet mouthpiece. The carved recess should resemble the interior shape of a trumpet mouthpiece, as shown.

To Play
Use the same procedure as for the hose bugle, p36.

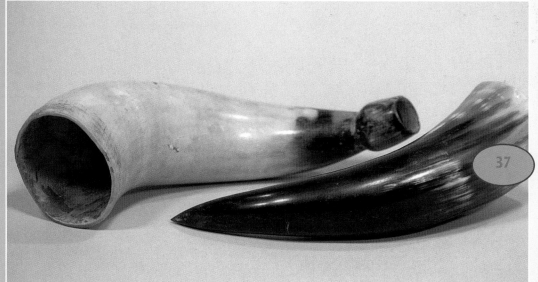

CONCH SHELL TRUMPET

A soft, eerie sound is produced from large shells. Smaller shells are more piercing.

Materials
One large sea shell

Tools
Grinding wheel or industrial-strength saw
Round file
Sandpaper

Assembly
1 Clean the sea shell inside and out.
2 Slowly grind or saw the tip of the spiral. **Note** Sea shell dust is harmful to inhale. Wear a filter mask.
3 Continue grinding until the opening is approximately the size of a dime.
4 Round all sharp edges with a file and sandpaper.

To Play
Use the same procedure as for the hose bugle, p36.

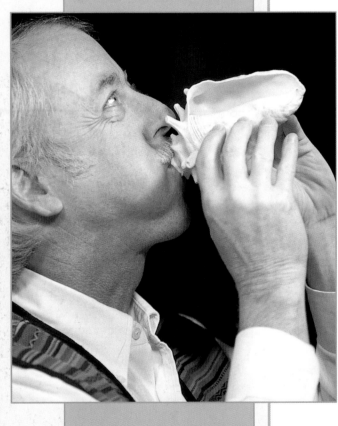

DIGERIDOO

The digeridoo is unique to the Australian aboriginal but has become popular worldwide. Traditionally made from a branch of eucalyptus tree that had been hollowed out by termites, digeridoos today appear in a variety of materials and styles.

Materials
1 to 1½ in diameter PVC or ABS plumbing pipe, 4 to 5 ft long
Optional style of plumbing pipe connector for mouthpiece
Bee's wax for mouthpiece

Tools
Pipe cutter or saw
Sandpaper
File

Assembly

1 Cut pipe to length. Try playing as a tuba.
2 Add extra plumbing mouthpiece, if necessary, to make a larger or smaller diameter. Smooth sharp edges with a fine file or sandpaper.
3 Apply softened bee's wax around the mouthpiece for lip comfort.

To Play
Buzz your lips very loosely. Aim for the lowest possible pitch. Consult a player who can show you some techniques such as circular breathing.

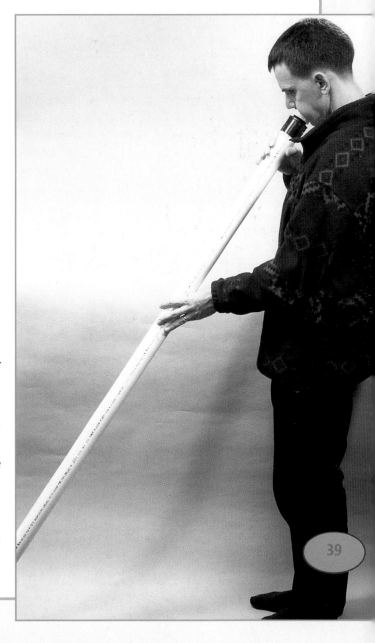

39

PERCUSSION INSTRUMENTS

Idiophones

Cymbals, gongs, and bells belong to the idiophone (self-sounding) branch of the percussion family. They are commonly fashioned from metal or wood, and vibrate in a complex fashion. Glockenspiels, chimes, and xylophones depend on a stiff bar, rod, or pipe for vibration. Shakers and rattles (maracas), scrapers and rasps (gulros), clackers (claves and castanets), jingles (tambourine), and many more do not produce a pure or recognizable pitch, but each instrument is capable of a number of tonal effects depending on how it is held, what it is struck with, and how it is struck.

All world cultures have instruments designed to be tapped or struck in some way. In Native American and African cultures, for example, these instruments are considered a necessity for ritual and ceremony. Percussion instruments that utilize stretched skins, vellums, and membranes are called membranophones. Drums are included here, and, as with strings, their pitch depends on the size and weight of the membrane and the amount of tension under which it is held. The loudness or amplitude of the sound depends on the force of the blow. The tone depends on the materials from which both the drum and the mallets or beaters are made. There is virtually no end to the combinations of sounds that can be achieved with percussion rhythm instruments.

Pounding a drum with an incessant beat can have a hypnotic and powerful effect on performer and listener. The complex patterns and layers of rhythms, called polyrhythms, are incredibly intense and compelling, as evidenced in many African and East Indian cultures.

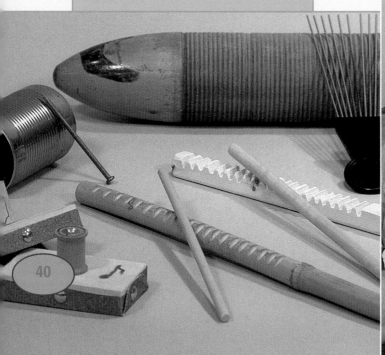

40

SHAKERS, SCRAPERS, AND STAMPERS

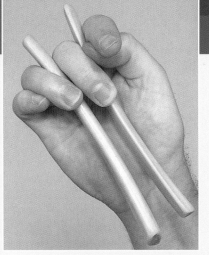

Rhythm Bones

Bones have a distinctive castanet-like sound capable of fancy syncopated rhythms. Proficient players can hold a pair of bones in each hand to give a startling performance.

Cow ribs are the traditional material, but hardwoods and softwoods can also be used. The usual length is around 6 inches. Bones from the butcher have to be boiled and scoured to remove residual sinue and grease. Polish with steel wool. Decorate them if you wish.

To learn the proper motion watch an expert. Or try holding the bones loosely on either side of the middle finger at about three-quarters of their length. The curved side of the bones face each other. The thumb-side bone is held stationary against the palm by the middle finger. The fourth finger adjusts the other bone to just the right proximity to its mate. The space and movement between the bones are actually quite minimal. The wrist is bent back slightly with the palm facing out. Throw your hand back and forth vigorously as if you were cleaning a window or waving goodbye. If done correctly, a triplet riff will happen. Then just keep it going.

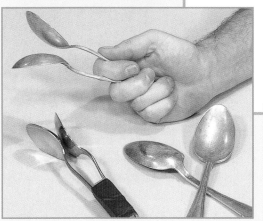

Spoons

Use two ordinary metal spoons (old soup spoons) or wood spoons to produce different effects. Place the spoons on either side of the index finger with the cupped sides facing away from each other and grab the handles firmly into the palm. There is actually very little space and movement between the spoons; rather, they are held tightly and controlled. Rattle them rhythmically between your thigh and your other hand. A down-down-up motion in a long-short-short rhythm is common in Appalachian music. Experiment with different-size spoons until you find the size and sound that suits you best.

Washboard

Washboards are another type of home-grown scraping and rubbing instrument common in the traditional music of the Appalachian Mountains and more recently adapted from the blues to zydeco. Use a washboard with metal ridges and a wire hair brush, a spoon handle, a stick, or any other scraper. Traditionally, players used two or three sewing thimbles for rubbing. Washboards often have optional attachments such as bicycle bells, horns, little cymbals, whistles, rattles, and some noisy, non-musical doodads. Attach the noisemakers with screws or glue. Make a simple harness to hang the washboard around your neck to free both hands for playing.

Then tap and rub along the metal ridges of the washboard in rhythm or jazzy syncopations. Use bells and horns sparingly for surprising, humorous effects.

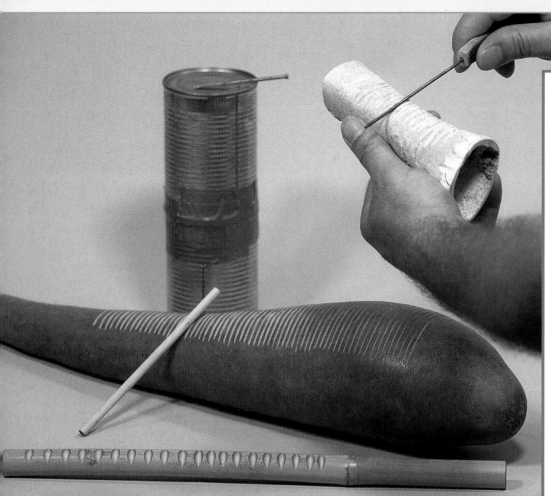

Scrapers, Rasps, and Guiros

To make these special effect music makers cut a series of grooves or notches in a wood or bamboo stick (into a gourd for a guiro) and rub across the grooves with a small-diameter wooden stick. The notches can be on one side or all around and can even be in patterns.

Try different rhythms and speeds. Place the end of the rasp on a turned-over bucket, washtub, or box to increase the volume. Listen for guiro rhythms, especially in Latin music.

Sandpaper Blocks

Sandpaper scrapers are often found in children's rhythm bands. Play by rubbing together harshly, softly, or in a circular motion.

Materials
2 blocks pine or plywood, 1 in x 4 in x 5 in
Sandpaper (medium grade)
Thumbtacks
Thread spools, cabinet knobs, or corks for
  handles

Assembly
1 Fold sandpaper over one side and edges of each block and fasten with thumbtacks. Cut out corners so sandpaper will fold neatly.
2 Trim off excess.
3 Glue or screw spool handles onto the uncovered side of each block.

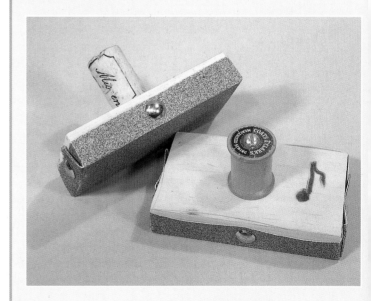

Rattles

Any container that can be sealed and easily handled will make a good rattle. And anything that will move freely inside the container completes the instrument.

Container suggestions
Soft drink, beer, or juice cans
Tennis ball can
Paper cups with lids
Any kind of plastic bottle
Small plastic or cardboard boxes
Plastic food jars
Gourds
Coconut shell
Balloons
Metal containers

Content suggestions
Rice or macaroni
Craft beads
Small rocks or pebbles
Marbles
Sand
Beans, seeds, or popcorn
BBs or buckshot

43

AFRICAN RATTLES

In parts of Africa, shells and beads held together by a loose woven netting were added to the exterior of a gourd or calabash for a sharp resonant sound.

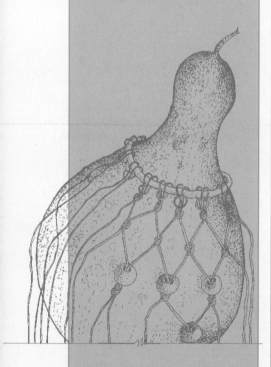

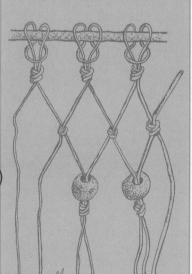

Materials
Medium-size gourd or plastic container with neck
75 ft of waxed linen cord
Short strip of rubber or rope
100 medium-size beads (plastic, wood, glass), shells, or large plant seeds

Assembly
1 Make a ring using a short strip of rubber, thin cord, or braid around the neck of the container. Secure.

2 To determine the length of each waxed linen strand, measure the distance from the collar to the end of the container, add 4 in, and multiply by 4.

3 The number of strands you need is determined by the circumference of the container. Use an even number and put one strand every ¼ in around the neck.

4 Fold each strand in half and mount it to the collar using a lark's head knot, as shown. Secure this knot with a simple overhand knot or granny knot, as shown.

5 Take one strand from each of two adjacent pairs and at approximately ½ in from the first knot tie another overhand knot, as shown. Continue this around the circumference of the container.

6 Add a bead onto the next row of adjoining strands and tie another knot to secure it. Continue in this way until all the rows of beads and knots are complete and cover the container almost to the bottom.

7 At the end, after the final row of knots, gather all the strands together and tie them, using a big overhand knot. Leave enough slack so that the beads are not too tight or loose.

To Play
Shake.

RAIN STICK

Depending on the material of the tube container and inside elements, various kinds of rain-like impressions can be created with this instrument.

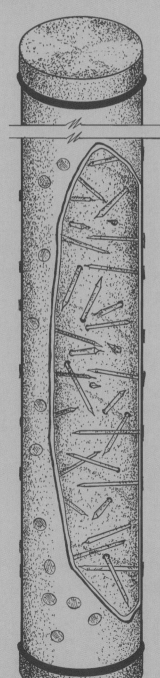

Materials
1 to 3 in diameter bamboo or cardboard tube, 1 to 3 ft long
Caps to cover the ends
Nails or wood splints
Rice, pebbles, seeds, or beans

Tools
Hammer
Tape
Magic marker (optional)

Assembly

1 Hammer or push nails or splints into chosen tube. The pattern of these creates the rain sound when the tube is turned over, and the rattling material finds its way through the nails from one end of the tube to the other. More nails generally produce a finer, longer effect. For bamboo or thick-walled tubing, pre-drilling holes is necessary.

2 Securely cap and tape one end.

3 Depending on the size of your rain stick, pour in enough rattling material (from list on p43) to fill tube about one-quarter of the way.

4 Cap and tape the other end. Wrap with tape if nails loosen.

5 Decorate, if desired.

To Play

Turn tube over and listen to the rattling material travel from one end to the other. Then turn tube over again.

DANCING BELLS AND JINGLES

Combine bunches of small bells, seed pods, animal hooves (most often goat), little shells, bottle caps, or other synthetic objects so they hit and sound against each other. Sometimes, these instruments are attached to the bodies of the dancers to enhance the rhythmic beat. Native Americans, East Indians, Africans, and most Middle Eastern cultures use bells attached to an ankle or arm for this purpose.

Materials
4 or 5 small spherical Christmas-type bells
2 in x 6 in leather strap
Leather lace or string

Tools
Sharp knife

Assembly

1 For each bell make one pair of slits spaced evenly across the leather strip with one slit at each end.

2 Thread lace or string through the end slit and through the first of the slit pairs. Thread a bell onto the lace and pull the lace through the other slit. Repeat. Leave enough lace at each end to tie around your ankle or arm.

Option Sew bells onto an elastic band or thread bells onto a leather lace and tie a single knot as you thread each bell. Tie finished product around your wrist, ankle, knee, or hold it and shake rhythmically.

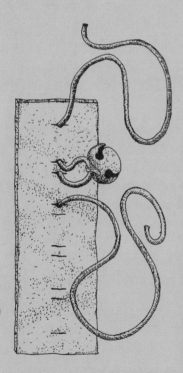

JINGLING JOHNNIE

Elaborate jingles probably originated in Turkey for use in military exercises. Eventually this instrument made its way through Europe and the United States. Shake it or tap it on the floor.

Materials
Rubber foot for chair leg or cane
Broom handle
Metal bottle caps
Round-headed nails, 1½ in
Options   Bells, cymbals, bicycle horns, drums

Tools
Awl or nail
Hammer

Assembly

1   Using an awl or nail, punch hole through center of each cap.
2   Nail caps along length of stick in a pattern of your choice. All caps should be loose enough to shake.
3   Put a rubber foot on bottom of stick to soften pole. Strike on floor.
4   More bells and jingles can be accommodated if cross pieces are attached to the main pole. Or hang bells around the rim of a tin can and attach the can to the pole by poking a hole through the bottom of the can and inserting it onto the pole.

To Play
Thump rhythmically against the floor and shake in the air.

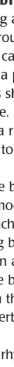
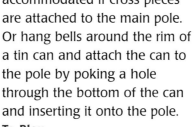

SLAP STICK

This instrument sounds like the cracking of a whip. Sticks are clapped together for the sound.

Materials
2 flat sticks
Leather hinge
Glue
Tacks

Assembly

1   If desired, cut a handle on sticks, as shown, for better control.
2   Glue and tack the leather hinge in place so that the two sticks make optimum contact when clapped together.

To Play
Clap together. Control the motion of the loose piece with your thumb.

STAMPING TUBES

Stamping tubes probably date back to prehistoric times and are still used today by various tribal cultures throughout the world.

Materials
Several feet of 1½ in diameter or larger PVC pipe
Matching caps or stoppers to close off and tightly seal one end of each pipe
Adhesive

Tools
Sharp knife, or saw

Assembly

1 Cut tubing to these lengths to produce a five-note scale, G to D.

G – 69 in	B – 54½ in	D – 46 in
A – 61¾ in	C – 51½ in	Note This is only one possible scale pattern

2 Fit caps tightly to end of each tube. Plumbing pipe stores will carry the appropriate cap or stopper to match piping. Special adhesive may be necessary to completely secure caps.

To Play
Drop each tube from about a foot off the ground onto its closed end. Dropping it onto a firm but slightly cushioned surface (thin carpeting) will give the best results.

RHYTHM STICKS AND CLAVES

Use various sizes and lengths of wood doweling, different spoons, segments of bamboo, broom handle sticks, plastic tubing, bones, tree branches, metal rods or pipes, or old railroad spikes for rhythm sticks. If you use sticks, strike the sticks (of different sizes and materials) to determine which ones resonate best. Experiment with different lengths. Sand the edges or corners round. Decorate, if desired.

Claves are a special kind of rhythm stick used in Latin music to provide the foundation beat (also called clave). Cuban music in particular uses the claves to maintain the groove in popular dance styles like the mambo, rumba, and cha-cha.

Assembly

1 Cut two 6-in segments of ¾ to ⅞ in hardwood doweling.
2 Sand and decorate.

To Play

Cradle one clave in your left hand and tap with the other stick. If you cup the left hand slightly and hold the stick loosely it will produce a more resonant sound.

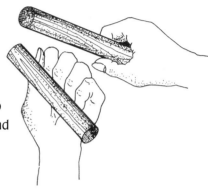

49

Simple chimes can be tuned to a scale or randomly pitched and can be sounded either by striking and shaking or hanging as wind chimes.

Ringing, bell-like sounds remind us of cathedral bell towers and church chimes. Also, tubular bells are often part of the symphonic orchestral percussion section. Surprisingly, these sounds can be produced from homemade models.

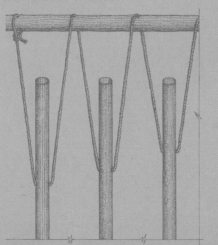

Wind Chimes

Materials
Large nails, tin can lids, pieces of glass, scraps of metal, strips of wood, segments of bamboo, lengths of metal tubing, flat sea shells, pieces of plastic, or old keys
String
Option   Wood or metal frame

Tools
Drill and bit

Assembly
Chimes are almost always suspended.

1 Drill a hole through each piece.

2 Attach to a string or suspend at intervals from a stick or wood disk. Also consider a round or triangular frame fashioned from wood or metal stripping.

To Play
To be effective, wind chimes should hang close together.

Suspended Chimes

Materials
½ to ¾ in diameter electrical conduit tubing or industrial tubing
Strong string, twine, or wire
Dowel or stick

Tools
Drill and bit
Hacksaw or tube cutter

Assembly

1 Cut tubing to desired lengths. Try the following suggested lengths.

$13\frac{7}{16}$ $13\frac{3}{4}$ $14\frac{3}{4}$ $15\frac{5}{8}$ $16\frac{5}{8}$ $17\frac{1}{8}$ $18\frac{1}{4}$ $19\frac{1}{2}$ 20 $21\frac{1}{4}$ $22\frac{7}{16}$ inch

2 Drill a hole in tube a little less than a quarter the length of the tube. Pass string through holes and suspend tube. **Note** Holes will be at different levels for different pitches.

3 Devise a way to suspend the tubes in a row at a convenient playing height, as shown.

4 Test pitches of scale with a wood or metal striker.

5 Fine tune the pipes. Make the pitch higher by trimming off a bit of length. If the pitch of a tube is too high, you'll have to cut another piece slightly longer and save the shorter one for the next highest note. Home centers and hobby stores are the best resource for metal tubing.

> Try stainless steel, copper, aluminum, or brass tubing for different sound characteristics.

Indonesia and Southeast Asia have large gong orchestras. Although ancient Chinese gongs were made from stone, metal, and ceramic, suspended clay flowerpots produce a surprisingly charming sound for a homemade gong orchestra.

This delightful looking and sounding instrument is modeled on a gong arrangement common to some East Asian cultures. The size of the bowl determines its pitch level. Softer beaters are better and will elicit a gong sound quality.

Flowerpot Gongs

Materials
Clean, unglazed, earthenware flowerpots
Heavy cord or twine
Mallet or striker (medium hard is best, see p65)
Pole or broomstick to suspend pots

Assembly
1 Size and thickness of flowerpots determine the pitch. Pick the pots you need to form a scale.
2 Tie a large knot in cord and insert it through drainage hole in the bottom of each pot, suspend pots upside down, and tie cord to a broomstick or other suspension framework. If the cord is too thin for a good-sized knot, tie it to a small piece of wood or doweling before threading it through the drain hole.
3 See p65 for striker ideas. Use medium-hard mallets for best tone. A rubber band wrapped around a macrame bead glued to a dowel works great.

Mixing Bowl Gongs

Materials
Several sizes of aluminum mixing bowls
Length of rope
Soft mallets (see p65)

Assembly
1 Drill a hole in the center of the bottom of each mixing bowl.
2 Arrange each bowl onto the rope, as shown, by tying a knot in the rope at appropriate intervals to achieve the proper vertical spacing.
3 Suspend the apparatus at playing level.

To Play
Strike gently with soft mallets.

51

TUNED GLASSES

Choose glasses and jars of many sizes (the finer the glass, the nicer the tone). Then all you need are some lightweight wooden strikers and water to put in the glass containers.

Vary the pitch by adding different amounts of water in each glass. To make a scale, start with an empty glass and add water, then work down the scale note by note as you add more water to other glasses. Thin-walled and crystal glasses have particularly pleasant tones. Adding water to a glass *lowers* the pitch. Songs and scales can be worked out easier if you work with the same style and size of containers. Try soft and hard mallets for striking (p65).

On fine glasses, especially crystal glass, a dampened finger rubbed around the rim will create a sustained singing sound. Around the region of Tibet, monks play their meditative "singing bowls" using this same principle.

Choose soft or hard mallets for striking.

52

XYLOPHONES

Xylophones are found in cultures throughout the world. They use bars of different sizes (long equals low, short equals high) to make different pitches. Most xylophones amplify their sound by coupling with tuned resonators attached to each key or bar. Xylophone keys may be constructed of wood, metal, bamboo, ceramic, and glass. The earliest examples, found in prehistoric burial sites, are made of stone. The xylophone family includes the Latin American marimba, European glockenspiel, African balafon, and instruments of the Indonesian gamelan orchestra.

A xylophone from 2x4 boards, available at any hardware store or home center, is easy to make, sounds great, and requires only a saw. It's large enough to accommodate two or more people playing.

2 x 4 Xylophone

Materials
2−2 in x 4 in boards (aim for no knots and no cracks or splits) for keys
Lengths of pipe insulators or any other soft or spongy material for supports

Tools
Saw

Assembly

1 Cut lowest key 3½ ft long.

2 Place it on spongy supports at nodal points (see p55) and test with an appropriate mallet.

3 Tuning will be done later, but if you wish to lower the pitch of any key, make a simple cut into the underside in the middle of the key. To raise the pitch, cut it a little shorter.

4 Each key thereafter should be approximately 2 in shorter than the one before, depending on the type of scale. This measurement will increase in the low range and decrease in the high range. Note Every piece of wood has its own tone and pitch characteristics.

5 Using the techniques suggested in step 3, adjust the tuning of keys as needed.

6 Try different types of mallets (p65) for various textures.

53

Arrange wood sticks on a simple framework and play. Metal pipe (though quite different-sounding than wood) works just as well. Some care is needed to tune the keys and insure a good scale, but the fun of playing is worth the extra effort.

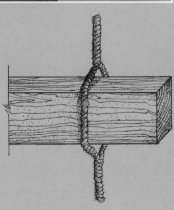

Hanging Wood Xylophone

Materials
1 in x 2 in piece of knotless softwood or hardwood several feet long
4 or 5 ft heavy twine
Wooden strikers (see p65)
Option Stapler and staples

Tools
Saw
Sandpaper
Scissors

Assembly

1 Measure the wood (see p55 chart for suggested lengths) and mark off the desired lengths. Start with 1 to ½ in increments. There will be less contrast between key lengths as the pitches go higher (and the keys get shorter) in the upper register. Fine tuning will be done later but make adjustments as you see fit.

2 Lay bars out from longest to shortest on a length of twine laid in a U shape. This is a convenient way to arrange the bars for initial testing and tuning.

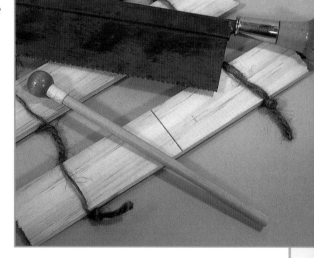

3 Tap the longest bar until you get a clear sound. You will need a quiet place.

4 After rough-cutting the next longest bar, tune it to the second scale degree by sawing a little bit off the end to make the sound higher or by a shallow cut underneath the bar at the midpoint to make the pitch lower. A little cutting can make a lot of difference, so proceed carefully. Experiment on a scrap piece of wood first.

5 Continue with each piece until the entire scale is cut and tuned.

6 Now tie knots at each loose end of the twine. Mount the bars by untwisting the twine just enough to push the bar ends through the separated strands. The strands of twine should encircle each bar at the nodal point (see sidebar, p55).

7 Continue to insert each key at an appropriate spacing. Stabilize by stapling the twine to the back of each key.

8 Hang arrangement or lay on a table for playing.

9 Make a couple of mallets appropriate to the size of your hanging xylophone, see p65 for mallet suggestions.

54

This instrument is more complex than the hanging xylophone. It works on the same principles, but has keys arranged on a wood framework.

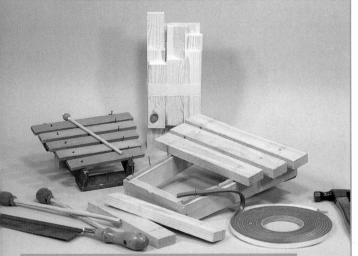

Wood Xylophone and Stand
Materials
15 ft clear (no knots or splits) softwood or hardwood for keys

1 in x 3 in softwood, 5 ft long, for frame stand

Glue

1½ in finishing nails for assembling frame

2 in finishing nails

Thick rubber bands or 4 ft of thin plastic tubing or weather stripping

Mallets (see p65)

Tools
Hammer

Saw

Drill and ⅛ in bit

File

Sandpaper

Clamps

Assembly
1 To prepare the keys, plane wood to 1½ in wide and ½ in thick and saw each piece to prescribed lengths listed in the chart. Since different woods each have their own properties, there is no way to predict the exact pitches so some experimentation will be required. Use the tuning principles outlined for the hanging xylophone (shorter equals higher, longer or thinner equals lower—thinner can be achieved with a simple cut or scoop in the back center of a key). The wood xylophone can have any number of bars, but select the lengths in the chart sequence.

2 Drill a ⅛ in hole in each bar at one nodal point (see left sidebar). Sand smooth.

3 To make the frame, cut 1 in x 3 in wood into two 24 in lengths for side runners. The lengths of the two end pieces that complete the frame are determined by how the nodal points line up from the longest to the shortest key.

4 Glue and nail the end block pieces to the side runners, as shown.

For best results, keys should be from same board or a board with exactly the same density or thickness.

Cut pieces of wood to the following lengths:

16 in

15⅛ in

14⅜ in

14 in

13⅛ in

12¼ in

11⅞ in

11⅛ in

10½ in

10 in

9¾ in

9¼ in

A vibrating bar's nodes (points of minimal vibration) are 22% of the total length in from the ends, as shown. Support for the keys should touch only at the nodal points, allowing the rest of the bar to vibrate freely. Note   Drawing exaggerates actual bar movement for the sake of illustration. Also, the bars will sound best when rested on soft or spongy supports. If a key has a dull sound try changing the place at which it is touching the support. You will know when you've arrived at the nodal area for support because of the improved quality of tone when the bar is struck. If you make a permanent stand for the xylophone, the configuration of the nodes will dictate the measurements and proportions necessary to make a stand.

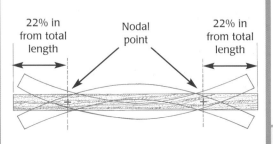

| 22% in from total length | Nodal point | 22% in from total length |

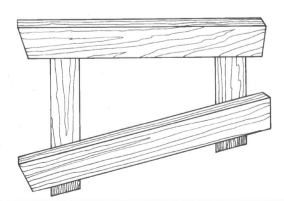

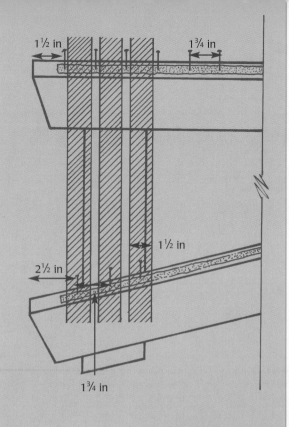

5 Starting 1½ in from the end of one runner, nail 2 in finishing nails down the runner at 1¾ in intervals.

6 Starting 2½ in from the end on the other runner, nail 2 in finishing nails at 1¾ in intervals. Note   Nails are started at different distances from the end of each runner so they will be in juxtaposition. The nails go through each wood bar on one runner, and fit between the wood bars on the other side, as shown.

7 Option   Enclose stand with a bottom piece of wood for more resonant sound. Sand and finish the stand. More sophisticated xylophones have separate compartments or resonating tubes beneath each key which are specifically tuned to the various pitches.

8 Rubber bands hitched along the nails on each runner will keep the bars from resting on the wood frame, thus producing a clearer sound. Small diameter plastic tubing or thin sponge weather stripping glued along each runner will give the same results.

9 Use hard mallets, p65, to produce a sharp clear tone.

Alternative stand for tubular xylophone creates very good tonal quality.

This beautiful sounding instrument belongs to an ancient family of pitched metal idiophones called metalophones (instruments that achieve sound through vibrating metal). In Indonesia, these pitched percussion instruments have been developed to a high degree as evidenced by large orchestras of tuned gongs, cymbals, and bronze and steel xylophones. Xylophones with metal bars are now found throughout the world. This xylophone project is made from utility metal tubing, available at most hardware stores.

Pipe cutter

Tubular Xylophone

Materials

½ in electrical conduit (aluminum alloy, steel, copper, or brass), 11 ft long
1 in x 3 in softwood, 5 ft long for frame stand
Glue
1½ in finishing nails
¼ in doweling, 2 ft long
Long rubber bands
Mallets (see p65)

Tools

Pipe cutter or hacksaw
Saw
Hammer
Files

Cut tubes to the following lengths:
14⅝ in
13⅝ in
13 in
12½ in
11¾ in
11⅛ in
10¾ in
10¼ in
9¾ in
9⅛ in
8¾ in
8¼ in

Assembly

1 Cut piping into prescribed lengths, as shown in chart, using a pipe cutter or hacksaw. Use this chart as a general guide. Fine tuning may be done as you cut each length or after the instrument is assembled. The tubular xylophone, like the wood xylophone, can have any number of tubes, but select the lengths in sequence.

2 The pitch may be sharpened by filing or grinding a bit off the end of a tube. However, if the pitch goes too sharp, it is best to cut a new length and use the old tube for the next highest pitch. Make sure sharp edges are filed smooth.

3 To make stand, cut 1 in x 3 in stock into two 24 in lengths for the runners. As with the wood xylophone, the degree of convergence of the runners as the keys progress from long to short is determined by the alignment of the nodal points on the tubing (see p55).

4 Glue and nail the end pieces to the runners, as shown.

5 Drill ¼ in holes along top edges of runners, leaving 1¾ in between holes.

6 Cut the ¼ in wood doweling posts so that 1 in remains above each hole. Glue dowels in holes and let dry.

57

Stringing detail

7 Sand and finish stand.

8 Suspend tubes between posts by placing the end of a large rubber band over an end post, twist it once, insert pipe into the rubber band, twist again and begin the process again around the next post. Use several small rubber bands if long ones are not available.

9 Repeat step 8 along other runner. Arrange tubes so that they are graduated symmetrically based on the arrangement prescribed by their nodal points.

10 Make soft and hard mallets (see Drumsticks and Mallets, p65). Experiment with different kinds of mallets. Use two, three, and four mallets simultaneously for chording.

This unique and unusual percussion instrument is played in parts of Southeast Asia and elsewhere. The Vietnamese variety is called a k'longput. The easy availability of large bamboo in Asia encourages the development of these instruments. In North America, we use PVC plumbing pipe.

Materials
Several feet of $1\frac{1}{2}$ in diameter or larger PVC pipe
Option   Matching caps to close off one end of each pipe. This lowers pitch exactly one octave.
Flip-flop sandals or other medium-hard paddles for slapping the open ends of each pipe
Option   Plywood and lumber for a stand

Tools
Saw
Basic woodworking tools

Assembly
1 Mark the desired lengths along pipe (see table for chromatic scale).

2 Slapping the end of the open tube will sound a specific pitch depending on tube length. Cap one end of tubes for a sound that is one octave lower.

3 Percussion tubes are most easily played when mounted on a stand, as shown. Cut the necessary number of holes in a piece of plywood through which the pipes will hang. A collar of tape around each pipe will keep the pipes from falling through the holes. Devise a way to suspend or support the whole apparatus at the correct playing height.

4 To play, slap the open end of each pipe with a dense foam or light rubber paddle (flip-flop sandals).

G	$34\frac{5}{8}$ in
G#	$32\frac{3}{4}$ in
A	$30\text{-}\frac{3}{4}$ in
A#	$29\frac{3}{8}$ in
B	$27\frac{1}{2}$ in
C	$25\frac{3}{4}$ in
C#	$24\frac{1}{4}$ in
D	$22\frac{7}{8}$ in
D#	$21\frac{3}{8}$ in
E	$20\frac{1}{8}$ in
F	$18\frac{5}{8}$ in
F#	$17\frac{7}{8}$ in
G	$16\frac{7}{8}$ in
G#	16 in
A	15 in
A#	14 in
B	$13\frac{1}{4}$ in
C	$12\frac{1}{2}$ in

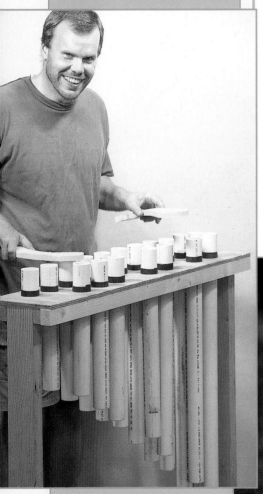

THUMB PIANO

This unique instrument is modeled after the African mbira (also called sanza, likembe, and kalimba). Thumb pianos come in all shapes and sizes with any number of keys. Some varieties are held inside a large gourd or other container for added resonance. This arrangement also enables the sound to return to the person playing the instrument. Africans often add bits of metal, shells, and other things onto the instrument that rattle and buzz in response to the playing to make the sound more interesting.

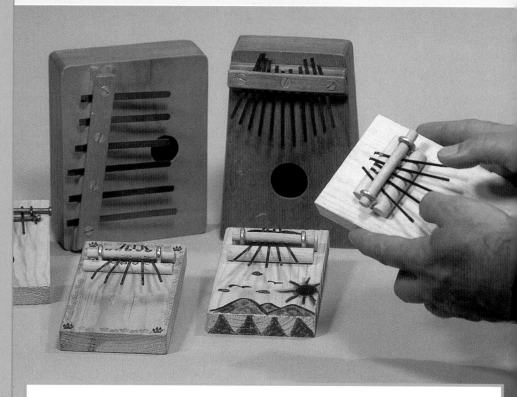

Materials for thumb piano keys Leaf rake tines cut to 3 in to 4 in lengths work well, or use flattened steel or spring steel. Coping saw blades cut to length work nicely but you will need to file away the saw teeth. Huge bobby pins and bicycle spokes have also been used. Or use bamboo splints filed to about ⅛ in thick or popsicle sticks.

Materials
Wood strip 24 in x 2 in x ½ in for sound box frame
2 pieces of 7 in x 5 in x ⅛ in plywood for top and
  bottom
2 strips 6½ in x ¼ in x ¼ in wood (or 2−6½ in
  lengths of ¼ in doweling) for bridges
2 strips 6½ in x ¾ in x ⅜ in wood (or 2−6½ in
  lengths of ⅜ in doweling) for securing keys
3 or 4−1¼ in screws
Springy tongues of metal or wood for piano keys
Finishing materials

Tools
Small wood saw
Hacksaw or tin snips
Drill and bit
Hole cutter or
  coping saw
Screwdriver
File
Glue
Clamps

Assembly

1 Saw 24 in x 2 in x ½ in strip into four pieces: 2−7 in lengths and 2−4 in lengths, for the sides of the sound box.

2 Glue and clamp side pieces to the 7 in x 5 in x ⅛ in plywood back and let dry.

3 On the top soundboard plywood piece, pencil the placement of bridges, as shown (p61). Leave at least ¼ in between bridges. Pencil 1½ in diameter sound hole centered and 3 in from end opposite bridge, see photo, p61.

4 Make sound hole with a drill hole cutter, or cut out with a coping saw. Sand smooth. More ornate sound holes are suggested in appendix, p120.

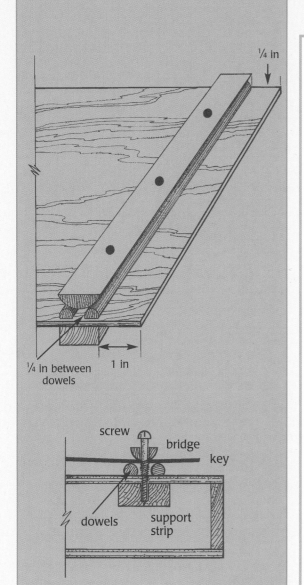

¼ in

¼ in between dowels

1 in

screw

bridge

key

dowels

support strip

A simpler form of thumb piano can be constructed by attaching the keys to a thicker soundboard and bypassing the sound box construction (see photo, p60). Resonance and volume are then enhanced by placing the soundboard onto a resonating surface such as a cardboard box or desk top. Once the principle of how the bridges are arranged for maximum sound production is understood, you can invent your own method of attaching the keys.

5 Glue bridges into place.

6 On other side of plywood (inside of box), pencil the placement of supporting strip of wood so that when bridges and support block are glued in place they will look like the cross section drawing. Glue and clamp into place.

7 Place the 6½ in x ¾ in x ⅜ in down-bearing strip of wood between the two bridges, hold firmly, and drill pilot holes for the screws. Pre-drilling will prevent the wood from splitting as the screws are tightened. The hole size in the interior supporting strip should be just slightly smaller than the screw size, and the holes in the down-bearing strip should be larger than the diameter of the screw.

8 Glue the top assemblage to the sound box. Clamp and let dry.

9 Trim, sand, and finish.

10 Cut tongues to varying lengths (approx. 3 to 4 in for metal). Sand off all sharp edges and corners and place tongues at even intervals across box.

11 Carefully screw the down-bearing strip on top of the tongues until they begin to produce a clear pitch. Leave them slightly loose for tuning.

12 Before the screws are tightened snug, adjust the tongues to match a scale by varying the length of the vibrating portion.

To Play

Hold the thumb piano in both hands, as shown, with thumbs plucking the tongues singly or in combinations to make melodies or rhythmic ostinatos.

61

PERCUSSION INSTRUMENTS

Membranophones

Drums usually have two components: body and membrane. Some drums, such as many Native American tom-toms, have two skins, one on top and one on the bottom; Latin American conga drums or Irish bodhrans have only one skin; while concert kettle drums have one skin stretched over an enclosed bowl. There is an endless variety of styles and sounds produced.

Drum Body Suggestions

Drum bodies, round or square, also called drum frames or drum shells, may be made from sturdy tin cans of any size, clay pots, rigid boxes, kitchen bowls, kegs, buckets, tubs, packing cartons, industrial containers, sewer pipe, construction tube used for concrete pilings, cardboard carpet tubes, etc.

Drum Head Materials and Methods

You can use rawhide animal skin (preferred), or synthetic materials such as heavy packing or other thick paper (sometimes used with cloth reinforcing), rubber inner tube tires, modern vellums, plastic packing tapes, stiff cardboard, rubber from large balloons, tin can plastic lids, strong cloth, thin plywood, reinforced mailing tubes, shrink wrap, and plasticized paper. These synthetic drum heads are highly resistant to weather and changes in humidity but need some sort of tensioning mechanism to pull head tight enough for good sound. Use standard commercial drum hardware for snare drums and conga drums from your local music store. It's safer to buy the hardware first and then design the drum shell to accommodate it or use lacing and toggles. The early American revolutionary-style drum used this method.

Rawhide   Untanned animal skin (rawhide) comes in different weights or thicknesses. Commercially processed hides are prepared to a uniform thickness by the manufacturer. Goat and calf skins are all-purpose choices. Thick cow skin is reserved for only the stoutest of drums. If available, skins from deer and elk also make excellent drums.

Cut the skin at least 2 in larger than the drum frame. Soak in cool (not hot) water for an hour or two (longer for thicker skins). Place the skin onto the drum frame while it is wet. Do not pull the hide tight at this point. Concentrate on tacking, lacing, or banding (p63) it firmly so that it is even and smooth around the head and has no major wrinkles. The skin will shrink as it dries. Let the skin dry slowly for a full day before attempting to play the instrument.

Note   Natural skins respond to changes in humidity. On rainy, damp days, skins will go flaccid making them ineffective for playing. Gradually heating the drum head will retighten the hide. Be careful not to overheat. If the head becomes too tight on very dry, hot days, sprinkle with water to loosen the skin.

Cloth   Canvas, duck airplane cloth, muslin, percale, heavy linen, or modern tenting materials are suitable for cloth-faced drums. This does not use the paper vellum bonding agent but otherwise is constructed as paper head.

Paper   A light-duty homemade drum head can be made from heavy paper (grocery bags) combined with cheesecloth, muslin, or other substantial cloth. Layer the cloth and paper together with the paper on the outside of the drum. Cut the layers 2 in larger than the drum frame. Dampen the layers evenly to conform to each other, place them together on the drum, and carefully pull both layers even and taut. Secure by banding or tacking to the drum frame. You might anchor the cloth and paper temporarily with large rubber bands while securing. Let dry. Apply three or more coats of shellac, letting each coat dry thoroughly. The shellac provides rigidity and bonds the paper to the cloth. Play this drum gently; it will not withstand hard drumming, although it will produce a nice tone when tapped lightly.

Rubber Membranes Old automobile inner tubes, bicycle inner tubes, or heavy balloon rubber can be used. Cut the rubber about 1 in larger than the drum frame. Pull rubber tightly and tack, lace, or band it onto the drum body. Several rounds of tightening are required to bring rubber to an appropriate tension. If you lace, be sure to punch the lacing holes with a leather punch to prevent tearing.

Plywood Wood tops work especially well when glued to a long resonator such as a large diameter, heavy-duty cardboard or plastic tubing, available at most home centers. Use standard $\frac{1}{8}$ in plywood or very thin specialty plywoods. Thin plates of wood resawn from solid stock work equally well.

Attaching Drum Heads

Tacking
Secure membrane head with long furniture tacks with decorative heads and paper and cloth drum head with short bulletin board tacks.

Banding
Use on drum shell with protruding lip around the edge and secure with heavy rubber bands, twine, string, or tape, or thread twine through holes punched around skin head at 1 to 2 in intervals. Thin strips of wet rawhide make excellent banding material because rawhide will shrink and tighten as it dries.

Commercial Hardware
Use on synthetic drum skins.

Lacing
With thicker skins punch holes with leather punch and use zigzag pattern of lacing sometimes incorporating toggles and wedges for adjusting. For thinner skins fold

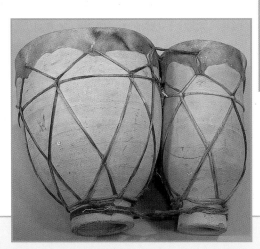

> Skins from smaller animals are useful for small drums. Possom, rabbit, groundhog, cat, dog , snake, lizard, and fish skins can be used.

63

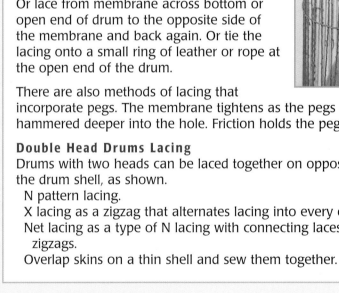

edge of skin over two or three times, punch holes, use grommets, and add a decorative touch. Or soak a thin tree branch or strip of wood in water and bend it into a hoop slightly larger than the diameter of the drum shell. Join ends of wood strip with a scarf joint and secure tightly. Or sew a length of string, twine, or rope into the skin. Whipstitch the skin onto the wood hoop or rope loop with a needle and string thread or fishing line. Punch holes at appropriate intervals around the skin for receiving the lacing.

Single Head Drums Lacing
Punch holes into skin and an equal number of holes into shell. Lace, as shown, with twine or leather thonging. Alternatively, a separate loop of lacing may be entwined through holes drilled around the shell. The membrane lacing is then zigzagged.

Or lace from membrane across bottom or open end of drum to the opposite side of the membrane and back again. Or tie the lacing onto a small ring of leather or rope at the open end of the drum.

There are also methods of lacing that incorporate pegs. The membrane tightens as the pegs are hammered deeper into the hole. Friction holds the pegs.

Double Head Drums Lacing
Drums with two heads can be laced together on opposite ends of the drum shell, as shown.
  N pattern lacing.
  X lacing as a zigzag that alternates lacing into every other hole.
  Net lacing as a type of N lacing with connecting laces between zigzags.
  Overlap skins on a thin shell and sew them together.

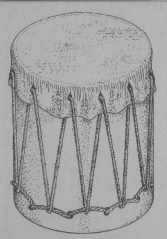

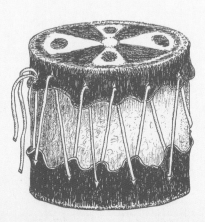

DRUMSTICKS AND MALLETS

Some drums are designed to play with your hands and others with various sticks and mallets. The striker you choose makes a big difference in the sound. Have a variety of mallets on hand with different degrees of hardness or softness. You can make your own or buy them at your local music store.

Simple Drumsticks
¼ to ½ in doweling of varying lengths
8 to 12 in chopsticks
Tree stems
Eraser end of pencils

Hard Mallets
1 Use a 12 in length of ½ in doweling. Carve a broad groove about ⅝ in from the end to make the tip. Sand the end round and finish. Make two.
2 Glue appropriate-size wood macrame beads onto matching dowels or sticks.
3 Wine corks, old cork fishing floats, or other corks carved or sanded into a round shape can be fitted and glued to a dowel or stick.
4 Hard plastic balls or thread spools can also be glued to dowels or sticks.

Soft Mallets
1 Use 12 in of doweling, wrap and wind yarn, jute twine, or rope as tightly as possible until it reaches a diameter of 1 in. Dab with glue and work the glue into the fibers. Hold for a few minutes. Let dry before using. Or, wind strips of felt around the end of a dowel dabbing with glue as you wrap.
2 Small rubber balls, super balls (compressed rubber), or large erasers carved to a round shape and drilled out to fit on the end of a thin dowel make excellent soft beaters.
3 Cork, plastic, or wood balls glued on a dowel and covered with felt, fur, leather, yarn, wool, or other cloth material make superb soft beaters. The covering may be either glued onto the core component or wrapped around tightly and tied just under the knob with string or lacing.

DRUM PROJECTS

This easiest of drum projects produces a resonant, attractive sound. Try out various kinds of mallets or hand strokes to find the best technique.

The friction drum is like the cuica of Brazil. It is unusual because it is not struck at all. Instead, a thin stick is attached to the membrane and stroked with a dampened cloth creating growling, laughing sounds, often heard in the samba, the national dance of Brazil.

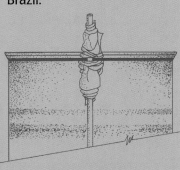

Packing Tape Drum

Materials
Clean 12 oz coffee can
Wide packing tape
New pencil with eraser
Decoration

Tools
Can opener
Scissors

Assembly
1 Cut out both ends of the can.
2 Stretch one strip of tape over can opening keeping moderate tension and secure to opposite side. Some bunching or wrinkling of the tape is likely but will not affect the final result.
3 Stretch another strip of tape at right angles to first strip. A third and fourth strip of tape should then fill in the open areas.
4 Trim excess tape around can and decorate with colored tape, stickers, or permanent magic markers.

To Play
Hold the drum up in the air and thwack the drum head with the eraser end of new pencil. Make a rhythm.

Tin Can Friction Drum

Materials
12 to 68 oz tin can
Thin bamboo skewer or ⅛ in wood dowel
Duct tape
Small piece of cloth

Tools
Awl or nail
Marking pen

Assembly
1 Use the metal bottom of the can or a plastic lid as the drum head (plastic lid is recommended for smaller can sizes).
2 Use the awl or a nail to punch hole in center of drum head for stick to just pass through.
3 Pull stick inside can so only 1 in protrudes on the outside of the can. Mark this spot.
4 Remove stick and wrap several tight layers of heavy tape around the stick at the mark.
5 Reinsert stick and wrap several layers of tape around protruding portion of the stick. The stick should be snug to the drum head with almost no slippage as you gently push and pull the stick from the inside.

To Play
Wrap a small dampened piece of cloth around the stick, apply gentle pressure on the stick, and stroke the stick with a push-and-pull motion. Vary the pressure until it makes a sound. Stroke the stick in a rhythm.

A twirling drum is used in some Buddhist ceremonies for meditation, in Africa for dancing, and throughout the Caribbean as a fun toy. Play it using a rapid twisting motion.

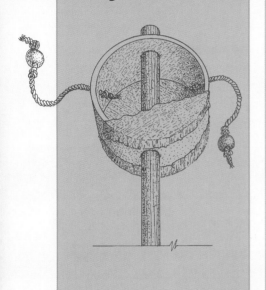

Twirling Drum

Materials

3 ½ to 4 in diameter carpet tubing, 3 in long for drum shell
Thin rawhide or other vellum to cover both ends of tube segment
String
2 small macrame beads
½ in dowel, 6 or 7 in long for handle
Thread or lacing materials

Tools

Drill and bit
Tacks or glue

Assembly

1 Drill ½ in hole all the way through tube. Insert dowel stick and secure with glue.

2 Attach strings to either side of tube and tie macrame beads to ends of string so they reach around and strike center of drum heads.

3 Cut two pieces of skin or vellum to size.

4 Secure skins to tube. Tacking or gluing will do for cardboard, paper, or skin vellums. Option   Sew or lace the two skins together (see p63-4).

To Play

Hold between your hands or in one hand and rotate rapidly. The beads should swing around striking each drum head, providing a fast repetitive rhythm.

67

Cluster different-size tin cans or plastic containers for a fun drum set.

Tin Can Drum Set

Materials
Several cans of varying sizes
    Heavy packing tape or duct tape
2 new pencils
Yarn or string for neck strap

Tools
Can opener

Assembly

1 Remove tops from cans. Leave bottoms intact.

2 Use largest container as center element and tape smaller containers around it. It is easier to tape the smaller containers together in pairs before attaching them to the larger container. Then tape each paired unit of containers to center can, one unit at a time. Secure with sufficient tape.

3 Attach a length of string for a neck strap.

To Play

Use the eraser ends of new pencils or other lightweight sticks to tap out rhythms.

some musicians like this configuration

Inner tube laced over a sturdy box, cake tin, can, or hollow cylinder such as carpet tubing, "Sono" tubing, large diameter pipes, or hollow logs make an effective drum.

Inner Tube Drum

Materials
Automobile rubber inner tube or other thin rubber membrane
Cake tin or other container, 3 or 4 in deep
Twine for lacing

Tools
Can opener
Utility knife or scissors
Marking pen
Paper or leather punch

Assembly

1 Use can opener to cut the ends out of the container.

2 Cut open rubber inner tube.

3 Lay tin onto rubber piece and draw a line around it 1 in larger than container. Repeat for second head.

4 Cut both circles with a utility knife or scissors.

5 At 1 in intervals punch (not poke) holes with paper or leather punch all around the edge.

6 Begin to stretch pieces evenly over the container and temporarily tie while you begin lacing and working your way around the container circumference. Since the tube should be moderately tight to give a proper tone, work your way around the drum several times tightening the lacing a little more each round.

7 Tie a good knot at the end and decorate heads, if desired.

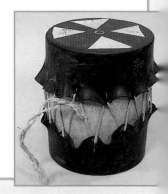

A slightly more sophisticated drum version requires a sturdy shell and rawhide.

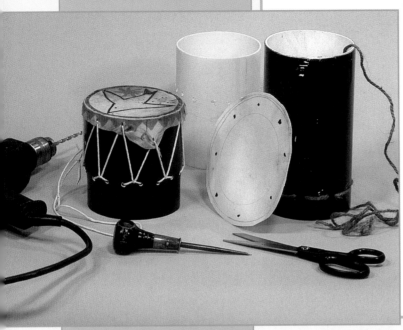

PVC Rawhide Drum

Materials
6 to 8 in section of 4-in-diameter PVC pipe
Medium-thick rawhide (goat or calf)
Strong string, twine, or thonging

Tools
Drill and bit
Awl
Scissors

Assembly

1 Drill eight equally-spaced holes around one end of the pipe.

2 Weave string in and out of the holes.

3 Cut rawhide leaving 2 in overhang and punch eight holes around periphery.

4 Soak rawhide for one or two hours.

5 Using an N lacing pattern (see p64), secure the rawhide to the end of the pipe opposite drilled holes.

6 Use several rounds of tightening to bring skin to desired tension. Don't stretch too tight, because skin will shrink as it dries.

7 Let dry slowly.

To Play
Use hands or small mallets for playing.

Slit drums have a single slit or cut from end to end. The two resulting lips on either side of the slit are thinned to varying degrees resulting in a difference in pitch. In Africa, slit drums are played in formulated patterns to achieve speech-like phrases.

Bamboo Slit Drum

Materials
1 to 2 in diameter bamboo
Mallets with hard knobs, p65

Tools
Drill and bit
Keyhole saw or coping saw
File

Assembly

Length of bamboo should include the natural nodes or joints at each end. Be careful not to splinter bamboo when cutting and drilling. Make sure tools are sharp.

1 Drill two $^{3}/_{16}$ in holes about 2 in from each end.

2 With the saw cut a slot connecting the two holes. You may need to widen the slot with a file to make sure the two resulting lips are well-separated from each other.

3 Be careful not to split the bamboo or you will have to begin anew.

4 Experiment with slots of varying lengths.

Ancient Aztec log drum or teponatzli was used in initiation rites and ceremonies. It was carved from a solid timber about 3 ft long. Many kinds of log drums are found throughout Africa and the Pacific.

This project uses a box construction.

Tongue Drum

Materials
2–14 in pieces softwood or hardwood, ½ to ¾ in thick and 3 to 4 in wide
½ to 1 in thick wood for sides and ends of sound box
Wood glue
Finishing nails or clamps

Tools
Saw
Keyhole saw, coping saw, or electric jigsaw
Drill with ¼ in bit
Hammer
Finishing materials

Assembly

1 Fit sides and end blocks to back.

2 Glue and nail (or clamp) sides and ends to the back, being careful to get a tight fit. Let dry.

3 Carefully draw the tongue pattern on top piece. Begin with a simple H design with each tongue a different length. A ratio of 3:4 usually produces a pleasing interval between the two opposing tongues.

4 Cut tongues in top before or after gluing it to the rest of the box. Strategically-placed holes drilled through the top at the tongue termination point will allow you to insert a saw blade and cut along the pencil lines until the H configuration is complete.

5 In the case of multi-tongued drums, create a series of Hs or tongues of unequal lengths across the top. Multi-tongue designs are more challenging and tricky to tune. Other interesting variations are to cut a different design into each facet of the box or incise more complex creative patterns into the top.

6 Sand off excess edges, round the corners, and finish.

7 Make mallets (see p65).

To Play
Strike with hard mallets and soft mallets to get the desired effect. Strike tongues in different places to find the most resonant spot. Placing the box on a spongy surface or lifting the box off the surface creates a richer tone. It will resonate more if you hold it in the air.

A hardwood top will produce a sharper tone than softwood. Pitch is determined by thickness and length of each tongue. Generally, the larger the sound box, the more resonant the tone and more definite the pitch. Use somewhat thinner wood stock for small boxes and thicker tops for larger boxes.

In place of rawhide drum heads you can use plywood. A larger drum head area and longer resonator (body) will result in better sound. Wood top drums are impervious to weather and never need tensioning. One interesting style of Afro-Cuban box drum called cajon is simply a 2-ft-square wood box.

Conga drums belong to a category of African- and Latin-based drums and are characterized by a long, conical or barrel shape drum body. Greater enclosure generally results in a more resonant sound, especially in the low range.

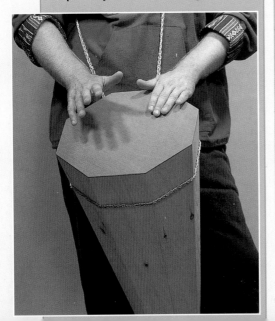

Box Drum

Materials
Plywood under ⅛ in thick (³⁄₃₂ in is best), or solid wood stock planed to this thickness
Glue

Tools
Tablesaw
Band clamps

Assembly
Construct a square box to desired dimensions.

Note   Gluing thin wood on almost any resonate container gives good results.

To Play
The player sits directly on top of the box and plays between the legs with the hands on one of the box faces. Striking different areas of the playing surface elicits a number of different high and low sounds.

Wood Top Conga Drum

Materials
Several feet of 1 in thick softwood, hardwood, or plywood
⅛ in thick (or less) plywood
Cardboard
Glue

Tools
Tablesaw
3 or 4 band clamps
Finishing materials

Assembly
1 Make a template from cardboard for side pieces of drum 2 ft long tapering from 5 to 2 in. Draw on wood.

2 Set angle of tablesaw blade to 22½ degrees.

3 Make a jig to hold wood securely.

4 Carefully cut eight tapered pieces.

5 Glue all the pieces together and hold with band clamps. This requires an extra set of hands to hold all the components together while adjusting and tightening the clamps. Let dry.

6 Cut plywood for drum head to dimensions of the drum shell and glue securely.

7 Trim and sand all excess material.

8 Decorate and finish.

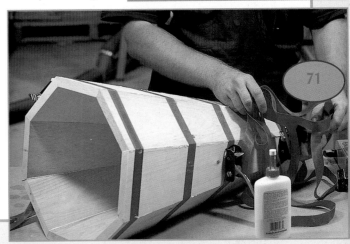

71

Combining two or more smaller diameter tubes of different lengths in a linear arrangement or cluster provides a more varied spectrum of pitches. This project describes simple bongos using cardboard tubing and thin plywood. Boobams are an extension of the bongo idea using more and longer segments of tubing.

Frame drums have a vellum (rawhide) attached to a frame that may vary in diameter from 6 to 18 in. Frame drums are usually circular, but square drums work just as well and are generally easier to make. Hoop drums usually require special procedures to bend the wood. Steaming cabinets or bending irons are common techniques (see bending iron, p101).

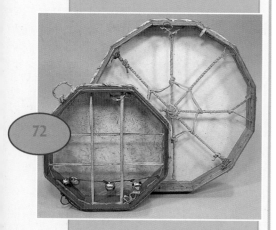

Bongos and Boobams

Materials
4 in diameter cardboard tubing, 2 ft long
1/8 in thick plywood (or less)
Screws and nuts
Glue or heavy tape

Tools
Utility knife or saw
Clamps
Drill and bit

Assembly
1 Cut tube into 2 lengths (8 in and 6 in)
2 Cut plywood for drum heads. Glue and clamp them to the playing end of each tube. It is easiest to glue heads before tubes are connected. Trim and sand.
3 Drill matching holes in sides of tubes and screw them together from the inside; or glue or tape them together.
4 Decorate and attach a neck strap.

To Play
Use your hands or mallets.

Hoop Drum, Frame Drum, Square Drum

Materials
1/2 to 1 in thick wood stock, 5 ft long, or sturdy round or square frame wood packing box
1/2 in finishing nails
Glue
Rawhide skin or other appropriate membrane
Long furniture tacks with decorative heads

Tools
Hammer
Scissors

Assembly
1 Saw 2–12 in lengths and 2–15 in lengths of wood. Make frame smaller, if desired.
2 Glue and nail drum frame together. Let dry.
3 Trim rawhide to shape with enough to wrap around and tack.
4 Soak rawhide in cool water for an hour or two. For thicker skins, soak overnight.
5 Tack rawhide to one side of frame, then pull skin around box so that skin overlaps the sides and is reasonably taut but not too tight. Place a tack about every inch.
6 Repeat on the other side. Tack skin along edges. Cut out corners so skin will be flat.
7 Let dry slowly overnight.
8 Decorate.

COMPLEX FOLK INSTRUMENTS
About Wood, Tools, Glue, and Tuning

This section introduces a variety of folk instruments of increasing complexity and sophistication. Beginning instrument makers, amateur craftsmen, and makers of folk instruments will find many useful ideas and suggestions to help them in all aspects of instrument making.

Wood for Stringed Instruments

Softwoods and the Soundboard

The soundboard (also called top or face) of stringed instruments is the most important area in determining the final sound. Traditionally, the best violin makers chose only German spruce growing between the trunk and first limbs on the south side of a tree that was growing on the south side of a mountain and cut it only in the depths of winter when the sap was down! The drying process was also important and it was years and even decades before the wood was deemed useful.

Today, as well as German spruce, there are a number of North American softwoods of excellent quality. For example, western red cedar, Canadian yellow cedar, blue spruce, and sitka spruce are used by major guitar companies everywhere.

Grain Configurations

The best soundboard wood has a long straight grain of parallel lines with minimal defects on the face and an end grain of vertical annual rings for strength and proper vibration. When preparing to make your instrument, search for this vertical grain pattern. Most wood cut in modern mills is whorled or irregular and the end grain passes from edge to edge rather than from face to face.

Wood in commercial lumberyards has already been dried in large kilns to a degree of usability. Nevertheless, be sure to inquire about how the wood has been dried and what moisture content to expect and allow it to cure further before you use it.

Note   Be aware that advertised wood dimensions are rarely accurate since wood is measured freshly cut and shrinks as it dries.

Plywood

Another alternative for soundboard wood is thin, high-grade commercially available plywood. It is stable and strong, doesn't warp, and is available in wide widths that don't have to be resawn from a plank into thin slabs and glued edge to edge for wider instruments.

The best plywood for plucked stringed instruments, Baltic birch, is usually imported from Europe and comes in a variety of thicknesses (number of laminates). Use three plys of very thin wood veneer commercially glued together to a $3/32$ in thickness. You can also use $1/8$ in 3-layer lamination with a good hardwood of maple, birch, or mahogany on the outside faces.

Resawing Solid Wood Stock

If you resaw, set up a guide wall or fence (2 in x 8 in board) parallel to the blade to hold the wood straight. Use a new $1/2$ to $3/4$ in skiptooth blade. Make sure the guide

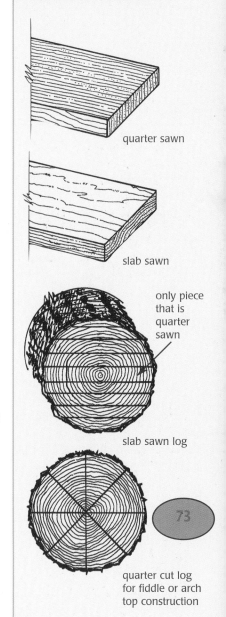

quarter sawn

slab sawn

only piece that is quarter sawn

slab sawn log

quarter cut log for fiddle or arch top construction

73

wall and blade are perfectly aligned to each other. Push the wood through slowly, keeping pressure against the guide wall. At the end pull it through with equal concentration. Then sand or plane to final thickness.

Hardwoods and the Sound Box

The back, sides, and neck of more expensive stringed instruments are made of hardwood such as rosewood, especially the Brazilian variety, or flamed or curly maple. Both are costly and difficult to work with for the novice. Beginning instrument makers can use mahogany and black walnut, or domestic sycamore, poplar, maple, cherry, beech, or birch. Imported hardwoods are available through specialty lumber and woodworking outlets.

Hardwoods and the Neck

Necks demand special care and should be quarter-sawn for maximum strength. This can usually be achieved by turning a slab-cut plank on edge so the grain will take on a more vertical configuration.

If quarter-sawn material is not available for the back and sides of a stringed instrument, use slab-cut back and sides that have been properly seasoned.

Humidity

• Wood expands when humidity is high and shrinks when humidity is low.
• 50% humidity is a good working atmosphere.
• Never glue or laminate on a rainy day.
• It is best to do your building in hot-dry or cold-freezing weather and not in a hot and humid environment.

Tools for Stringed Instruments

With a few exceptions, the main tools needed to build the instruments in this book are found in your own woodworking shop and are available at home centers and hardware stores.

Saws

For cutting straight lines use sharp tools—a tablesaw, radial arm saw, bandsaw, circular saw, or jigsaw.

Curved or irregular cuts can be made by hand with a coping saw or fretsaw. For larger jobs, use a bandsaw, jigsaw, or scroll saw.

Drills

Use a manual twist drill, brace and bit, power hand drill, or drill press.

Planes

Buy a block plane and jack plane to begin your hand plane collection. Scrapers and sandpaper are also useful for smoothing.

Knives and Files

Sharp knives, one or two basic chisels, and a mallet are useful for removing small areas of wood. Files come in a wide array of sizes and degrees of coarseness. For general use, I recommend a standard 8 in half-round wood file and an 8 in rasp for faster wood removal.

Clamps

Clamps make gluing and laminating easier and more effective. Use commercial clamps, large rubber bands or pieces of elastic, or heavy objects for

For solid wood stock body, follow resawing instructions. Use $^1/_8$ in hardwoods for back and sides and $^3/_{32}$ to $^1/_8$ in softwood for soundboard. You may have to glue plates edge to edge to achieve desired width. A book on guitar construction will provide you with the details for gluing and clamping.

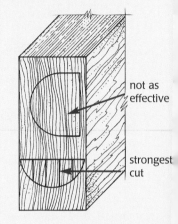

not as effective

strongest cut

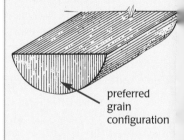

preferred grain configuration

weighting such as large bricks, stones, or scraps of metal. Always clamp or weight pieces first without glue to check for a good joint—then apply the glue and clamp. The more clamps the more even the bond. A bench vise or Workmate™ (Black & Decker) are also useful for holding your work stable.

Glues for Stringed Instruments

Cream-colored yellow aliphatic glues dry fast and hold extremely well. Both **white and yellow glues** are water-based so they will soften and yield their hold when in contact with water.

Hide glue is water-based and dries very slowly thus allowing for the positioning of difficult parts. It comes in natural (made from animal hooves and skins) and synthetic forms.

Epoxy glues come in fast and slow-drying varieties and form a bond that will not yield to water or heat.

Caution   Never use rubber cement or contact cement for laminating. These are useful only in veneering. Hot glue and krazy glue are used only under the most specific circumstances.

Tuning Suggestions

In order to make the best sound, your instrument needs to be fine tuned. Instructions on basic tunings for each instrument are included with the building directions. A piano, pitch pipe, or harmonica may also help get your tuning technique started. Begin by tuning the instrument as closely as you can to the designated notes, then go over the instrument again to fine tune it.

If the instrument is newly made, it may take a period of time for it to settle before the strings will stabilize and hold their pitches (especially the highly-tensioned hammered dulcimer and harp). Because of this, frequent tuning sessions will be necessary for a while.

DENNIS G. WARING,
INSTRUMENT MAKER
Middletown, Connecticut

APPALACHIAN MOUNTAIN DULCIMER

The origin of the Appalachian Mountain dulcimer is uncertain. We do know, however, that its North American manifestation came from European roots where there have been many dulcimer-like instruments. The oldest of these seems to be the German scheitholt documented during the Middle Ages. Other dulcimer-like instruments were known in France (epinette des Vosages), Norway (langesleik), Holland (hummle), Iceland (langspil), and Sweden (humle). One thing that all these instruments had in common was a diatonic fretboard that ran most of the length of the instrument, a fretted string or two on which the melody was noted, and an additional set of drone strings. All the instruments were tuned modally.

As the Appalachian Mountain dulcimer developed in North America it took on its own characteristic construction of three or four strings on a bilaterally symmetrical sound box often in an hourglass or tear-drop shape. The project outlined here is a long, trapezoid shape known for its ease of construction.

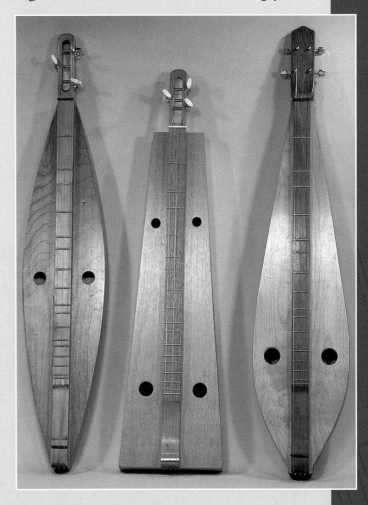

The Appalachian dulcimer is, in fact, more of a zither than an actual dulcimer, a term meaning sweet sound, usually reserved for the hammered variety. The name continued to be used over the years and was fixed in folklore so that now the Appalachian Mountain variety is usually prefixed with a "plucked," "fretted," or "lap," to differentiate it from its hammered namesake. Sometimes it is even called a hog fiddle.

The fretted dulcimer may be picked, plucked, feather quilled, bowed, or struck depending on the tune and desired style. Therein lies the charm of most all folk instruments. They can be played in any way you wish so long as the music pleases the ear.

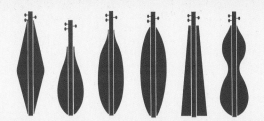

Materials
Poster board
Sheet of ⅛ in plywood, 2 ft x 3 ft for sound box
32 in x ¾ in x 1⅜ in stick of hardwood for fingerboard
12 in x 2 in x 1 in hardwood stock for two end blocks
Ebony wood, plastic, or bone for nut and bridge
Tuners
Strings
Fret wire

Tools
Bandsaw, jigsaw, or coping saw
Planes and chisels
Tape measure and rulers
Small square and sliding T-bevel
Files and sandpaper

Assembly

Initial cuts

1 Using measurements on p79, make a pattern on poster board and cut out. Transfer pattern onto ⅛ in plywood and cut out top and back. If plywood has a tendency to warp be more careful when clamping the glued parts.

2 Either cut the top and back separately or tape the top and back pieces together for more efficient cutting. Saw about 1/16 in outside the penciled line with a coping saw, bandsaw, or jigsaw. Do not cut inside the line.

3 Find the exact center line on the top and back plywood blanks and mark both pieces. The final sound box dimensions will span 4 in at the head and 8 in at the tail. At the head of the instrument, measure 2 in out from the center line in each direction and mark. Likewise, to define the width of the sound box at the tail, measure 4 in out from the center line. Complete the outline by connecting the top and end marks.

4 For the instrument sides, measure and cut the remaining plywood into two identical 26 in x 2 in pieces.

5 Cut two end blocks from a piece of hardwood. End blocks must be exact height of side pieces. End block at head of instrument should measure 3¾ in long, 2 in high, and 1 in thick. The end block at tail of instrument should measure 7¾ in x 2 in x 1 in. The end blocks now need beveling on the ends to accommodate the trapezoidal trajectory of the sides. Using a sliding T-bevel, transfer the necessary angles to the end blocks. Cut and file or sand smooth.

Step 1
Make dulcimer pattern

Step 2 Cut dulcimer back and top from plywood

Step 5 Bevel ends of end blocks cut from hardwood

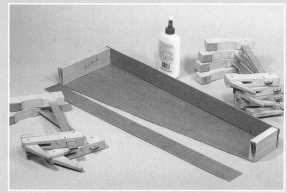

Sound Box Mock-up and Assembly

6 On the back, assemble the end blocks and sides without glue. Check the fit and make necessary adjustments.

7 Glue and clamp end blocks to back. Check along all joints making sure everything fits properly.

8 After glue dries on end blocks, place side pieces into position making sure they are the same exact height as end blocks. File, sand, or plane, if necessary. Apply an ample bead of glue along the bottom edge of each side and on each end of end blocks. Glue one side at a time. Clamp carefully. Check all joints for good contact.

Fingerboard

9 The fingerboard should measure 31 in x 1⅜ in x ¾ in. Using bandsaw and file, cut out the strum hollow about ⅛ in deep. Smooth with sandpaper.

10 **Option** Hollow out fingerboard to enhance sound. With a table saw or router, make a trough ¾ in wide and ½ in deep, and stop 6 in from the end that will be the tuner peg head. Start cuts from the end with the strum hollow and lift the wood, or stop the saw at a visible pen mark on the fingerboard. Since this is a difficult cut and not mandatory for a good sounding instrument, only experienced woodworkers should attempt it.

Peg Head

11 Draw peg head slot onto fingerboard according to diagram. Either drill out terminal points with a ¾ in bit and complete with a jigsaw, or drill out entire slot area on a drill press and finish by filing it uniform. Sand the entire fingerboard smooth. Note It is critical that the entire length of the fingerboard be perfectly flat.

Nut and Bridge

12 The scale length (inside measurement between the nut and the bridge) is 25¾ in. Measure and mark the position of the nut and bridge carefully. The nut should be just in front of the peg slot and the bridge just beyond the strum hollow. Make the nut and bridge ¼ in thick and ½ in high from bone, ebony, hard plastic, or any hardwood. Cut a ¼ in deep slot across the fingerboard with an appropriate saw to hold the nut. It should fit snugly into the slot. Do not glue yet. You can also make a slot for the bridge, but you may wish to have a floating bridge that can be adjusted after stringing the instrument in order to correct any intonation difficulties.

Steps 6, 7, 8 Prepare, glue, and clamp end blocks and sides to back

Step 10 Cut out strum hollow from fingerboard

Step 11 Drill peg head slot on drill press and cut out remainder of peg head slot on jigsaw

78

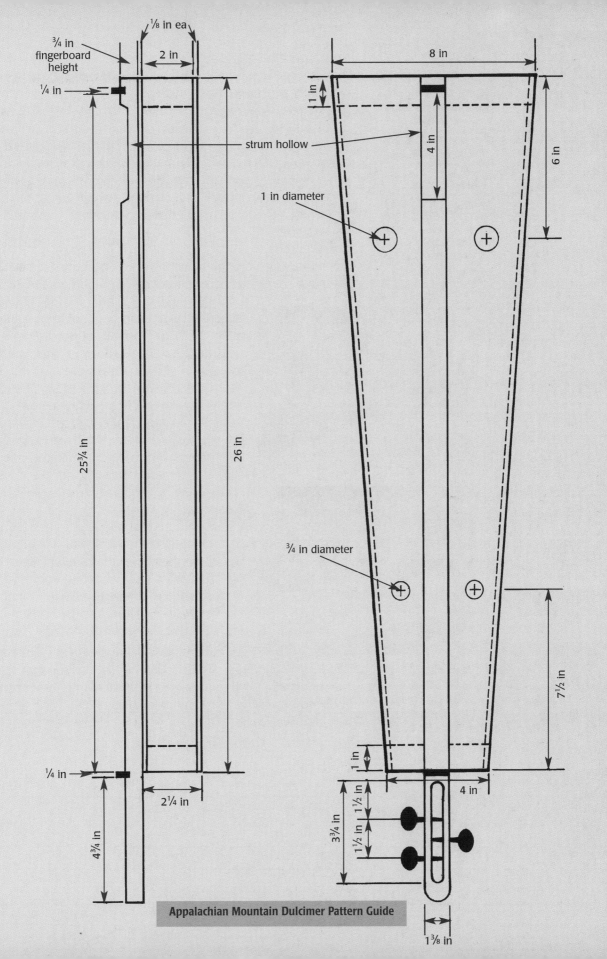

Appalachian Mountain Dulcimer Pattern Guide

¾ in fingerboard height

⅛ in ea

2 in

¼ in

25¾ in

26 in

¼ in

2¼ in

4¾ in

8 in

1 in

strum hollow

4 in

1 in diameter

6 in

¾ in diameter

7½ in

1 in

4 in

3¾ in

1½ in

1 in

1½ in

1½ in

1⅜ in

Scale and Fret Slots

13 Using a small square, accurately measure and mark the fret positions, as shown.

14 At your local music repair shop, buy 3 to 4 ft of fret wire and a saw that has a set to its teeth that matches the requirements of the fret. For me, banjo fret wire works best for dulcimers, but guitar wire is all right, too. Sometimes fine and extra-fine coping saw blades will cut a slot that will hold the fret snug. Some instrument makers buy a fine-toothed dovetail saw and carefully grind down the set of the teeth on a whetstone to just the right degree.

Fretting

15 Practice on a scrap piece of wood first. Cut each shallow slot just deep enough to receive the tine of the fret, as shown. Cut frets slightly longer than the width of the fingerboard and clip or file off excess after they are all in place. Carefully but firmly tap each fret into the slots, as shown. To help start the fret into the slot, place a piece of wood on the fret, and hammer the wood to set the fret firmly into the slot. Speciality hammers are available for this step. If the fret gets bent in the process or the slot is too big to hold it tightly, remove the fret, straighten it or cut a new one, and glue it neatly into place with epoxy glue.

Dressing the Frets

16 With a long, straight ruler check to see that all the frets are level with one another and of uniform height. If not, carefully lay a large file or fine sandpaper glued to a long flat stick on top of the frets and gently work them level. File the ends of the frets, as shown, until they are flush with side of fingerboard.

Round the ends of each fret with a fine metal file or fine sandpaper. Study existing fretted instruments to get the right shape. Run your fingers carefully along the edges to check for sharp tips that might nick fingers. Polish the frets using fine steel wool.

Fret Number	Inches from Nut
1	2.8094 in
2	5.3122 in
3	6.4593 in
4	8.5639 in
5	10.4390 in
6	11.2983 in
7	12.8750 in
8	14.2797 in
9	15.5311 in
10	16.1046 in
11	17.1570 in
12	18.0945 in
13	18.6242 in
14	19.3125 in
15	20.0148 in
16	20.6406 in
17	20.9273 in

Step 13 Mark fret placements on fingerboard using T-square

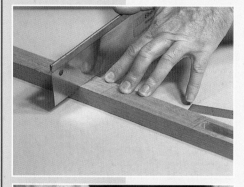

Steps 14, 15, 16 Cut fret slots with a backsaw, hammer frets into fingerboard slots, and file ends of frets

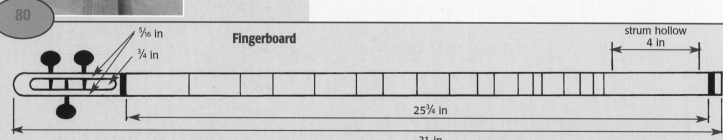

Fingerboard

5/16 in
3/4 in
strum hollow 4 in
25 3/4 in
31 in

Peg Holes

17 Drill holes into the peg head to match your tuners. Use three or four strings. (3-string dulcimer is more traditional and easier to play; 4-string features a double melody string course and has more tone). Do not attach the tuners permanently at this stage.

Soundboard Assembly

18 Place fingerboard directly down the center of top (soundboard) piece and mark each end for position. **Option** If you have hollowed out the fingerboard, you can further enhance the tone of the instrument by cutting a matching slot in the soundboard to duplicate the fingerboard slot, thus allowing the vibrations easier access into the sound box.

Sound Holes

19 Measure for placement of sound holes and drill circular holes into top, as shown. I have drilled the lower sound hole with a 1 in spade bit and upper hole has a ¾ in diameter. When using a large drill bit, be sure to clamp the work down firmly. Arrangements of circles of different sizes and fancy sound holes are options. Heart shapes are traditional (see Appendix). The size or placement of sound holes on simple folk instruments are not bound by any acoustic necessity, but become more important as instruments become more sophisticated.

Fingerboard to Soundboard

20 Position fingerboard again on soundboard and check line-up. Make sure peg head is extended beyond one end. Prepare clamps. Apply glue along the fingerboard, carefully place it onto the soundboard, and hold tightly for a minute or two. Do not let it slide out of line. Clamp and let dry.

Completing the Sound Box

21 Fit the top assembly onto the sound box and check for all around contact. Plane, file, or sand uneven spots. Sign instrument on inside, if you wish. Apply an ample bead of glue completely around the top edge of the sound box. Carefully position the top onto the sound box and hold tightly for a couple of minutes. Apply clamps or rubber bands all around the edge. Let dry.

22 File or plane away overhanging edges. Be careful not to chip the edge of the plywood or put deep scratches in the sides. Sand all the

Step 17 Drill holes for machine head tuners

Step 19 Measure for sound hole placement and drill holes

Step 20 Glue and clamp fingerboard to soundboard

Step 21 Level sound box components on a sanding board in preparation for gluing on the soundboard

---

Fret placement for different scale lengths

You can find your own fret placements for other scale lengths by using the rule of eighteen (or the integer 17.817). This formula will result in a chromatic scale (semitones). By leaving out the chromatic frets 1, 3, 6, 8, 11, 13, 15, 18, 20, 23, 25, and 27, you will have a diatonic (do-re-mi . . .) scale, appropriate for the dulcimer. Divide the string length by 17.817 to find the distance from the nut to the first fret (which the dulcimer doesn't use). The remaining distance divided by 17.817 gives the distance from the first fret to the second fret (which the dulcimer does use). And so forth. The twelfth fret should lie halfway between nut and bridge and the fifth fret halfway between the nut and the twelfth fret.

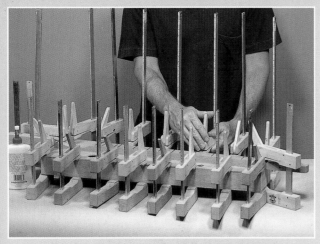

Step 21   Glue and clamp soundboard to sound box

Step 25
Attach
tuners to
fingerboard
peg head

Step 26
Drill holes
for hitch
pins

Step 27
File string
slots in the
bridge

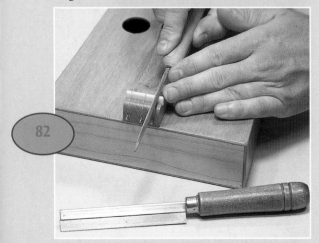

edges and corners slightly round.

23   Beginning with medium-grit sandpaper, sand out all scratches, rough spots, and glue smears. A sharp chisel may be needed to remove dried glue from corners and crevasses. Carefully sand the entire instrument with finishing-grade sandpaper.

24   See Finishing Suggestions, p117.

Tuners

25   Place tuners onto peg head and mark where screws will secure tuners to head. Pre-drill the screw holes with a bit just slightly smaller than screws. Some tuners (inexpensive banjo tuners) require no screws. Fasten these as instructed by the manufacturer.

Hitch Pins

26   Install small finishing nails, piano bridge pins, or other contrivance for securing the strings into the end of the fingerboard. Pre-drill and hammer pins in leaving about ¼ in protruding.

Nut and Bridge

27   Mark the string spacings on top edges of nut and bridge, as shown. With a very fine saw or knife-file, cut slots at a slight angle on the nut to within $\frac{1}{32}$ in above the surface of the fretboard (or less deep if you have used fret wire with a high crown). For the bridge, slightly angled slots are cut to within $\frac{3}{16}$ in from the surface of the fretboard. If guitar fret wire has been used, the tolerances will be a little higher.

28   Use banjo or guitar strings with these string gauges:

   Bass string .022 in wound with nickel or brass winding
   Melody string and middle string .010 in or .012 in plain strings
Strings with a loop-end are generally more practical but depending on the size of your hitch pins, ball-end strings are quite workable.

29   Setting the action of a stringed instrument means to tweak the relationship between the nut, frets, and bridge to an optimum degree. Start by checking the depth of slots in nut. The strings should pass as close to the first fret as possible without buzzing. To set the slots on the bridge, the strings must pass as close as possible to the third and fourth fret without buzzing when the finger depresses the string at the next relative lower fret.

Most buzzes are caused by an uneven fingerboard or misfitted frets. If your fingerboard is warped, you may need to true the frets by filing them perfectly level then reshaping the crown of each fret with specialty files. If a problem occurs, figure out the cause, and take a common sense approach to eliminating it.

Step 27   File string slots in the nut

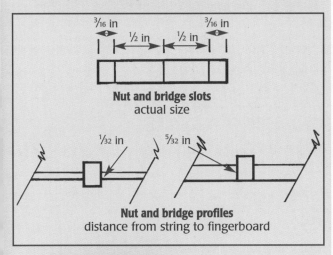

³⁄₁₆ in   ³⁄₁₆ in
½ in   ½ in

Nut and bridge slots
actual size

¹⁄₃₂ in   ⁵⁄₃₂ in

Nut and bridge profiles
distance from string to fingerboard

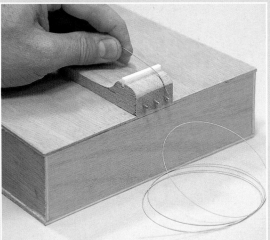

Step 28   String the dulcimer

Tuning the Appalachian Dulcimer

Find a quiet place and a comfortable chair with no arms. Put the dulcimer across your lap at a slight angle with the tuning pegs out towards your left knee and the tailpiece end next to your right hip. (Reverse if you play left-handed.) Tune the instrument to a pitch that sounds best. First tighten the bass string so that it has good resonance (pitch of C or D). Stringed instruments usually sound best tuned a little on the tight side. But never turn the tuning peg without simultaneously plucking the string so that you can hear how fast the tension is increasing.

After you are satisfied with the sound and feel, put a finger behind (to the left of) the fourth fret on the bass string. One by one tune all the other strings to this pitch. This may take a little juggling and adjusting, but do whatever is necessary to accommodate the fingering, plucking, and peg turning all at once. This will give you the Ionian mode, which is the same as the modern major scale.

The beginning of the scale or "do" is located on the melody string (closest to you) just to the left of the third fret. Keeping your finger close behind each fret, play up and down the scale only on the melody string while doing a simple strum across all the strings. A large thin pick is usually best for dulcimer strumming. Traditionally, players used a thin dowel as a noter instead of fingers. The noter is slid along the strings from note to note to produce a characteristic sound. Buy a beginner's dulcimer book for songs to play.

83

Originating a few thousand years ago in the Middle East the hammered dulcimer spread to Europe, China, and India in the 11th century. The Persian santir, Indian santoor, Chinese yang chin, Korean yangum, and Swiss hackbrett all belong to this branch of the zither family.

A late 19th century version, the Hungarian cimbalom, with a large chromatic range of four octaves and a string damping mechanism, incorporates the dulcimer principle (multiple string courses divided by bridges into different vibrating lengths) which led to the development of the piano.

English colonists introduced the hammered dulcimer into the United States during the 18th and 19th centuries. This lumberjack piano, as it was sometimes called, was portable, relatively maintenance-free, and could be easily moved from camp to camp.

Most hammered dulcimers have a two- to three-octave range capable of playing diatonically in three or four keys. Invariably, dulcimers are a trapezoidal shape and are designed to sit on a table or stand and are played with two small lightweight hammers or mallets.

The dulcimer in this project features a full treble bridge with three strings per course and an abbreviated bass bridge with two strings per course. If you wish to build a dulcimer with two complete bridges, simply extend the abbreviated bass bridge the full span of the instrument.

Materials

Poster board
¾ in plywood, softwood, or hardwood for the back
¼ in high-grade plywood, softwood, or hardwood for the soundboard
2 in thick maple or other hardwood for pin blocks
1 in thick maple or other hardwood for rails and bridges
Zither pins and matching tuning wrench
Music wire (.016 in, .018 in, .020 in, .022 in)

Tools

Bandsaw, tablesaw, or handsaws
Drill press
Jointer plane
Dremel tool and round bit
Coat hanger or small diameter metal rod
Hammer and awl
Clamps
Files and sandpaper

Step 1 Transfer pattern for back and soundboard to plywood

Assembly

Back and Soundboard

1 Make a full-size template pattern on poster board using measurements given on p87. Transfer pattern to plywood and prepare the back and soundboard blanks. Cut the back of the dulcimer from ¾ in stock and the soundboard from ¼ in stock to the dimensions shown. If you use solid wood stock, you may need to laminate two pieces edge to edge to achieve the necessary dimensions.

Side Pin Blocks and Front and Rear Rails

2 Wood for 3¼ in wide pin blocks should be sawed and planed to 2 in thickness. Maple hardwood will hold the great string tension but requires sharp tools. Softer hardwoods will work but are not as reliable. Pin block laminates used in piano construction are the best but expensive.

3 Lay pin block stock on the back piece of wood or use the template (p89) to draw lines at each end to delineate the form and length of each block. Cut one block for each side.

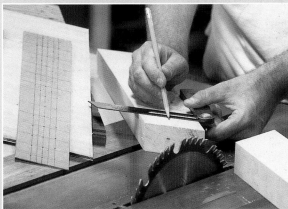

Step 3 Make pin blocks using template and tablesaw

4 From a 1-in-thick hardwood plank, cut two remaining components of frame so they measure 1 in x 2 in and fit between the two pin blocks.

5 Cut notches into each pin block using bandsaw or sharp hand saw. The 1 in x 2 in rails should fit snugly into the notches to stabilize the frame.

6 Glue and clamp pin blocks to the back. Spread a thin layer of glue on both gluing surfaces. Do not try to glue too many pieces at once. Use the 1 in x 2 in rails as spacers while clamping the pin blocks, then fit and

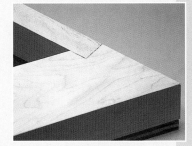

Step 5 Cut notches in pin blocks for front rail; detail of pin block and front rail juncture

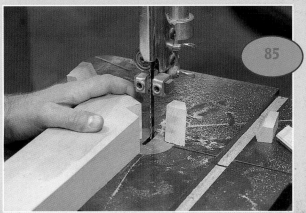

85

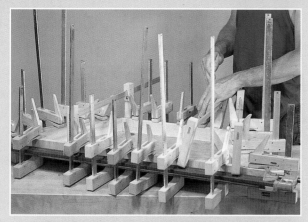

Steps 6, 7 Glue and clamp sound box assembly

Steps 8, 9
Mark interior
center brace
(treble); drill
sound holes in
braces, and glue
in place

86

glue the 1 in x 2 in rails in place.

7 Trim excess from around edges of frame on a power jointer or with a sharp hand plane.

Interior Braces

8 The box should conform exactly to suggested dimensions for precise placement of center brace. Glue it in the box at a ratio of 2:3 from the sides of the instrument. Once the strings are fitted, this ratio will produce the correct relationship between the left and right side pitches. If the dimensions on your instrument are different, check measurement on a pocket calculator. Fashion a brace ¾ in wide and same height as frame components. Drill large holes through the brace to connect the two sound chambers. Round the top of the brace. Glue in place and clamp.

9 Brace placement for bass bridge should be positioned at a reasonable distance from the right side, at a slight angle. Placement of this component is less exacting than the center brace. Drill a series of holes in this brace and glue to the back.

Soundboard Sound Holes

10 Place the soundboard on the sound box frame and draw lines for positioning of side bridges. Likewise, draw the position for center treble bridge and bass bridge on top of their respective braces. Now carefully drill a 2 in sound hole in each of the two areas delineated by the bridges, as shown. For more ornate sound holes make a pattern on heavy paper first and trace the shape onto the soundboard and cut out.

Top Assembly

11 Place the top onto the rest of the sound box and sand or file as needed for perfect fit. Spread a layer of glue around frame of sound box (tops of braces are usually left unglued). Place soundboard onto soundbox, position, and clamp. The more even distribution of pressure the better. Let dry completely. File and sand excess around edges after glue has set.

Side, Treble, and Bass Bridges

12 All the bridges can be fashioned from maple or hardwood left over from the other components. Cut groove (use Dremel tool) into each bridge top surface along its length for small steel rod or wire (coat hanger) to keep strings from cutting into wood and for better sound.

13 Side bridges rest on the inside edge of the pin block (3 in from the outside edge). Construction of the center treble bridge and bass bridge requires careful calculation. They have to be in perfect relationship to each other for strings to zig-zag correctly.

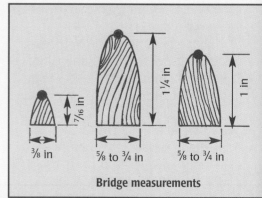

Bridge measurements

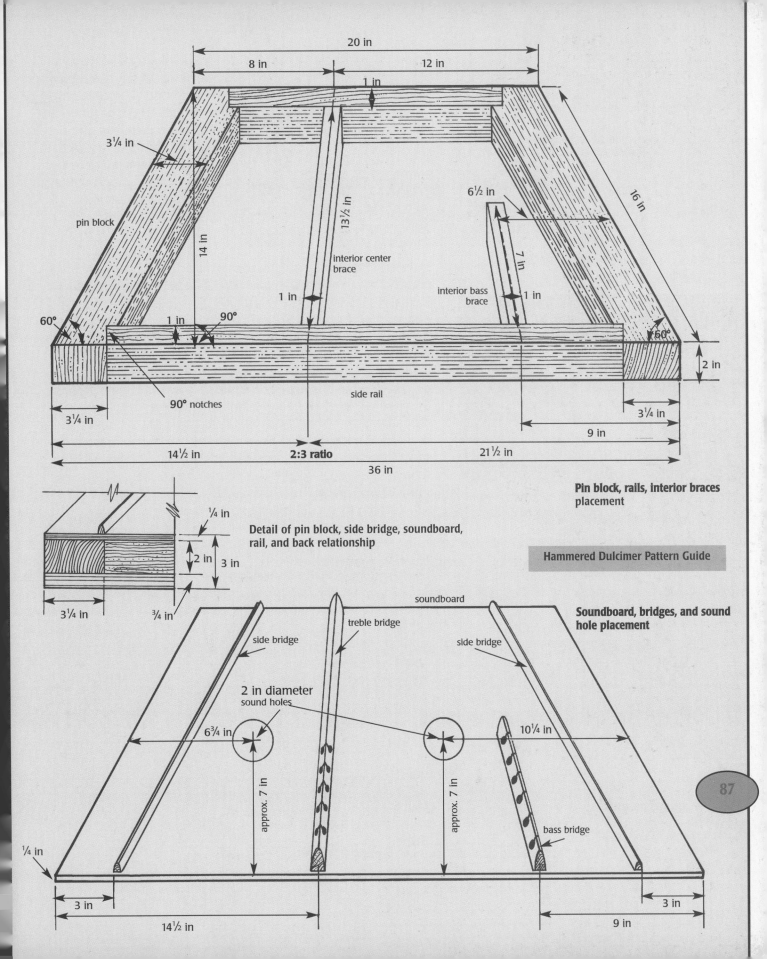

20 in

8 in · 12 in

1 in

3¼ in

pin block

14 in

13½ in

interior center brace

6½ in

16 in

7 in

interior bass brace

1 in

60°

1 in · 90°

90°

1 in

side rail

60°

2 in

90° notches

3¼ in

3¼ in

9 in

14½ in

2:3 ratio

21½ in

36 in

Pin block, rails, interior braces placement

¼ in

2 in · 3 in

Detail of pin block, side bridge, soundboard, rail, and back relationship

3¼ in · ¾ in

Hammered Dulcimer Pattern Guide

soundboard

treble bridge

side bridge

side bridge

Soundboard, bridges, and sound hole placement

2 in diameter sound holes

6¾ in

10¼ in

approx. 7 in

approx. 7 in

bass bridge

¼ in

3 in

14½ in

3 in

9 in

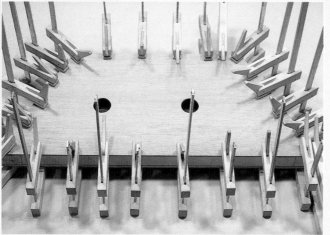

Steps 10, 11 Drill sound holes into the soundboard; glue and clamp soundboard to sound box

Step 12 Prepare bridge blanks; cut grooves into bridge tops with small hand router (Dremel tool)

See p90 for photo details of bridges

Draw a full-scale top view of the string scheme on the poster board master template for exact placement of zither pin holes and holes through the two main bridges. Use the tuning pin template provided (p89) to help you get started. Study drawings and photographs carefully to understand how the strings on the treble bridge pass through the bass bridge and how the bass strings pass through the treble bridge. This unique design allows for greater pitch range without increasing the size of the instrument. The tuning pin and hitch pin pattern on their respective pin blocks will determine the path of the strings and thus the position and angle of the holes drilled in the treble and bass bridges. Place the treble and bass bridges on your master drawing to check that the relationship between pin placement, string trajectory, and bridge holes all line up properly.

14 Drilling holes in the treble and bass bridges is potentially difficult and should be thought through carefully. Holes are angled to match the trajectory of the strings and drilling them requires a special setup depending on your tools and skill. Alternatively, separate individual bridges can be cut and positioned under each string course saving much calculation.

15 Fashion to the desired shape, as shown.

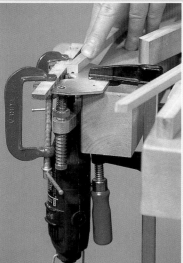

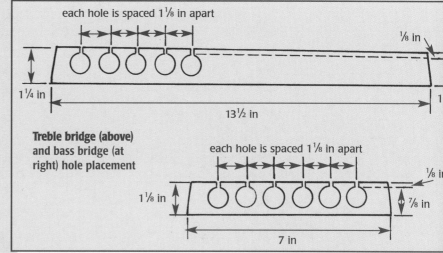

each hole is spaced $1\frac{1}{8}$ in apart

$\frac{1}{8}$ in

$1\frac{1}{4}$ in

$13\frac{1}{2}$ in

1

Treble bridge (above) and bass bridge (at right) hole placement

each hole is spaced $1\frac{1}{8}$ in apart

$\frac{1}{8}$ in

$1\frac{1}{8}$ in

$\frac{7}{8}$ in

7 in

Stringing diagram

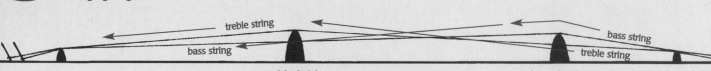

treble string

bass string

bass string

treble string

treble bridge

bass bridge

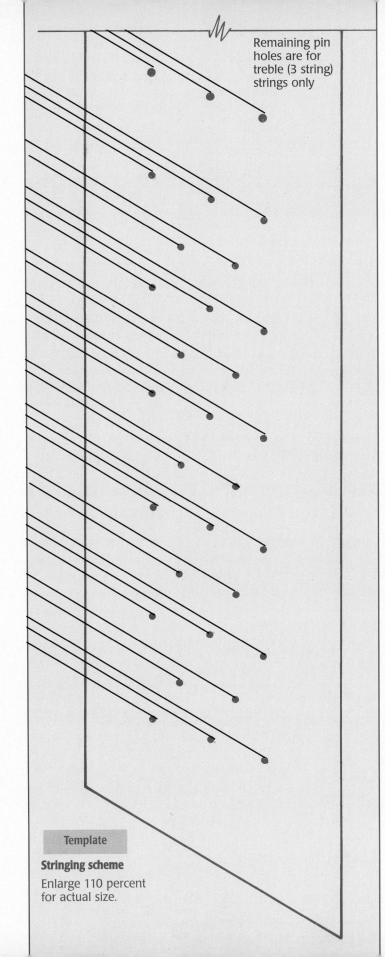

Remaining pin holes are for treble (3 string) strings only

Template

Stringing scheme

Enlarge 110 percent for actual size.

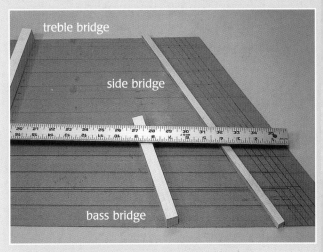

treble bridge

side bridge

bass bridge

Step 13 Plot and mark string trajectories and hole placements on bridges

Step 14 Plot and mark hole placements in bass bridge based on string projections

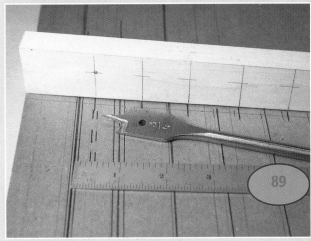

89

Step 14 Prepare to drill holes into bridges

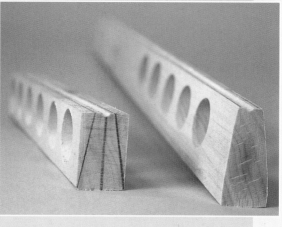

Step 15 Shape bridge with block plane; detail of bridge with holes; detail of bridge shaping

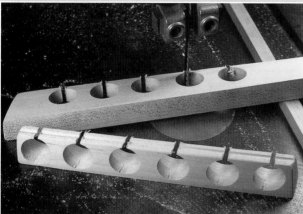

Step 16 Glue and clamp side bridge

Step 18 Mark tuning pin placement using template and awl

Step 19 Glue and clamp casing

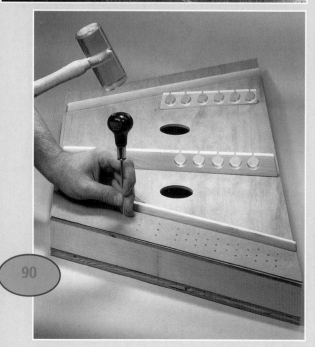

Bridge Placements

16 Carefully check placement of all bridges on the top. The side bridges are glued and clamped but not the center treble bridge or the bass bridge, which remain movable for accurate tuning as you string it up. The string pressure will hold these bridges in place. The center bridge placement in a 2:3 ratio between the side bridges produces the musical interval of a sol-do relationship called a perfect fifth. This means that there will be a five-note difference between the right and left side of the center bridge on each string.

Tuning Pins

17 Zither pins (and matching tuning wrench) are available through most music stores. It is crucial that holes for pins be drilled slightly smaller so pins will hold firmly. Test first on a scrap piece of hardwood. Most hardware stores sell drill bits in a spectrum of sizes. Take time to find a good match. The hitch pins (opposite the tuning pins) may be piano bridge pins, zither hitch pins, or 1 in finishing nails. For best results pre-drill holes before hammering pins in.

Tuning Pin Placement

18 Mark pin pattern on one side using an awl and flip pattern over for the other side. Drill holes for tuning and hitch pins using appropriate drill bits. Drill holes at a slight backward angle to keep string wound toward base of pin.

Case

19 Glue side panels around the instrument using any hardwood or softwood. An easier alternative is to veneer the sides of the instrument using hardwood veneers, a sharp knife, and contact cement. Follow directions on the can.

Finishing

20 Stain the instrument or finish with regular furniture varnish or polyurethane. Oiling with a modern furniture oil is also possible or spray with clear lacquer. (See Appendix, p117.)

Tuning Pins and Hitch Pins

21 Carefully hammer (or screw) tuning pins into pin blocks leaving enough pin protruding for the string to wind around. You will need a few turns for pulling the string taut later.

22 Hammer hitch pins into opposite pin block.

Stringing

23 Use British gauge number 6 (.016 in), number 7 (.018 in), number 8 (.020 in), and number 9 (.022 in) music wire (available at specialty music store or piano repair shop) to string your dulcimer. One roll of wire is usually enough to string several dulcimers.

24 Tie the end of each string, as shown, and string up a top and a bottom course for the treble bridge. Do the same for the bass bridge. Check all string alignments and make adjustments, if necessary. Add a few more strings and tighten to prescribed pitches. Adjust treble bridge placement so interval of a perfect fifth

Step 21 Insert tuning pins

Step 24 Put strings onto the dulcimer

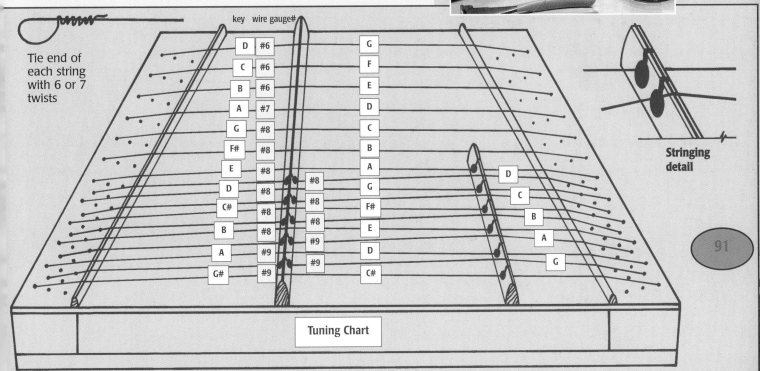

Tie end of each string with 6 or 7 twists

Stringing detail

key	wire gauge#		
D	#6		G
C	#6		F
B	#6		E
A	#7		D
G	#8		C
F#	#8		B
E	#8		A
D	#8	#8	G
C#	#8	#8	F#
B	#8	#8	E
A	#9	#9	D
G#	#9	#9	C#

D
C
B
A
G

Tuning Chart

is achieved between the two sides. Install all strings. Wind the strings close to the base of the tuning pins and hitch pins so they will pass over the side bridges securely and not buzz or shift.

Tuning

25 See Tuning Chart p91. Retune several times until it finally stabilizes.

Mallets

26 Mallets or hammers are anywhere from 8 to 10 in long. Glue felt or leather to face of each hammer for softer sound.

Playing the Hammered Dulcimer

Set dulcimer on a table and play it from either a standing or sitting level. Prop up in back to bring the higher notes closer to the player.

The trick to playing smoothly (especially in fast passages) is to alternate your sticking so that one stick does not play too many consecutive notes or that you do not have to cross your hands too much.

There are three major scales and their relative minor scales as well as other modal scales on the dulcimer. Consult a music teacher for music instruction.

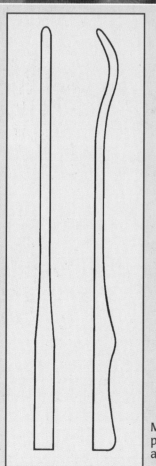

Mallet pattern (side and top view)

FIVE-STRING BANJO

Most scholars agree that the banjo is of African origin. There are, however, many examples of chordophones with skin-covered resonators found around the world. Nevertheless, it was enslaved Africans who brought the idea of the banjo to North America. In 1785, Thomas Jefferson noted that the "banjar" was the most popular instrument among American Negroes.

But a white American traveling musician, Joel Walker Sweeney, is given credit for developing the four-string tenor and plectrum banjos. His first five-string banjo is now on display at the Los Angeles County Museum in California. He even played banjo for Queen Victoria at a command performance. The development of the banjo continues today. Ol' time five-string banjos, bluegrass banjos, tenor banjos, and various hybrids continue to find an audience.

One of the most important historical banjo repositories is found in the Appalachian Mountain region of southeastern United States. The earliest banjos were built of hardwoods from nearby forests. The neck was shaped with a drawknife, spokeshave, pocket knife, rasp, and file. This was attached to a pot or wood resonator with a raccoon, squirrel, groundhog, cat, or some other "critter" skin laced over it. Tuning pegs were then carved and fitted into peg head holes which were drilled with an auger or reamer. Wire or gut strings were added and the banjo was ready for playing.

The five-string banjo project here is designed to be played in the traditional "flailing" or "clawhammer" style. Its overall wood construction produces an impressive sound and "has got the fun in it."

Step 1　First cut in neck stock to achieve angled peg head

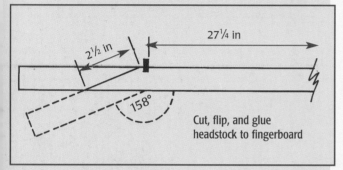

2½ in

27¼ in

158°

Cut, flip, and glue
headstock to fingerboard

Detail of flipping peg head stock under neck

Step 1　Glue and clamp for peg head

Materials

3 ft x 3½ in x ½ in hardwood board for resonator
36 in x 2½ in x 1 in hardwood fingerboard plank
10 in square ⅛ in plywood
25 in x 2½ in x ⅛ in hardwood for fretboard
4 machine tuners (several styles)
1 banjo fifth peg
Banjo fret material
Bridge and nut
5 hitch pins
Glue

Tools

Tablesaw or miter box
Bandsaw
Spokeshave
Drill and bit
Files
Sandpaper and finishing materials
Clamps

Assembly

Neck

1　On the 36-in fingerboard stock measure 27¼ in from one end. Allowing for ¼ in nut placement, on the 1 in edge side, measure and mark a diagonal. The angle cut for the headstock is variable. Examine existing instruments. Cut, flip, and glue the headstock to the fingerboard, as shown. To prevent slippage between parts try out a clamping process before applying glue and make sure everything fits properly. Then glue.

2　Transfer all designs for neck (p97) to neck blank. Draw top and side views onto the wood. You may wish to make an actual-size pattern of the fingerboard on paper first and then trace it onto wood. Make sure the fifth peg is on the proper side. Some left-handed players place it on the other side.

3　As you cut the neck out on the bandsaw, cut as much of one

Step 3　Cut sides of neck and peg head shape

profile as possible without actually cutting it completely off. Then cut the other facets and finally complete the initial cut last. Think through process carefully before cutting. Check thickness of the peg head remembering that a $\frac{1}{8}$-in-thick face plate will be added later. Saw neck to specification (p97). Saw out the peg head shape. Undercut the part of the neck that will be directly under the soundboard (see pattern, p97).

4   With a spokeshave and file, begin shaping the back of the neck. Be sure to shape to measurements indicated on pattern.

The Pot

5   Eight identically cut pieces (4 in x 3½ in) glued together form a frame-like pot. Set bevel to 22½ degrees. Outside measurement of each piece is 4 in. Cut the pieces with a tablesaw or a miter box to achieve the correct beveled angles so that all parts will fit.

6   Fit eight pieces together. Make any minor adjustments in the angled cut.

7   Cut a 1-in-deep notch for neck in one of the pot pieces, as shown.

8   Glue pot together using band clamps or heavy-duty rubber bands.

Soundboard

9   Place the pot assembly onto $\frac{1}{8}$ in plywood piece and outline with pencil. Cut out design being careful not to chip plywood.

Mock-up Assembly

10   Begin fitting neck/pot relationship. File as needed.

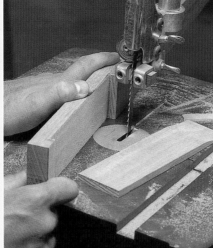

Step 3   Make an undercut in the neck to accommodate the soundboard

Step 4 Shape back of neck with a spokeshave, and smooth neck back with a file

Step 7, 8   Cut the neck notch in one facet of the pot; glue and clamp the pot together

Step 5   Cut the pieces for the pot on the tablesaw at a 22½ degree angle

Step 9 Cut out soundboard from $\frac{1}{8}$ in plywood to fit on pot

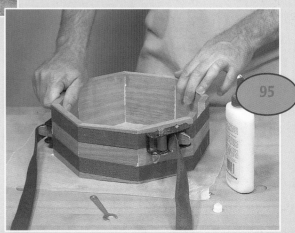

Step 11 Cut out peg head face plate, glue and clamp face plate to peg head

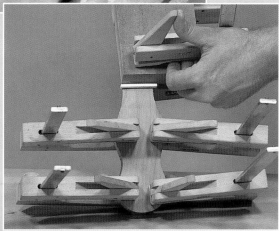

Step 12, 13 File peg head and face plate; drill holes in peg head for tuning mechanisms

Peg Head Face Plate

11 The thickness of the peg head plus a ⅛ in face plate should be calculated to accommodate chosen tuning mechanisms. The face plate will cover the joint seam peg head construction. Trace outline of peg head onto ⅛ in hardwood piece to make face plate. It is primarily decorative so select an attractive piece of wood. Cut out and glue to peg head. Let dry.

12 Shape and refine peg head. Carefully position machine head tuners on back of peg head and mark exactly where each tuner post will pass through peg head.

13 Using a drill bit slightly larger than the tuner post (usually ¼ in), drill the holes through the back of the peg head being careful not to chip the face plate as the drill passes through.

Fretboard

14 While ⅛ in fretboard stock is still in its rectangular form, starting from the position of the nut, clearly and precisely mark the placement of all the frets using the chart below. Placement is based on a scale length (distance between the nut and bridge) of 23½ in. (See "rule of eighteen" in Appalachian Mountain Dulcimer sidebar, p81)

15 Carefully cut the fret slots with a saw designed for this purpose.

16 Trace outline of actual neck onto the back of fretboard. Carefully cut out fretboard. It is usual to glue the fretboard to the neck without frets and install the frets afterwards. As you prepare to glue fretboard to neck, the relationship (measurements) between the nut, frets, and bridge must be precisely maintained in order for the instrument to play in tune. Glue and clamp fretboard to neck.

Fret Placement Chart	
Fret Number	Inches from Nut
1	1.3190 in
2	2.5639 in
3	3.7389 in
4	4.8480 in
5	5.8949 in
6	6.8830 in
7	7.8156 in
8	8.6959 in
9	9.5268 in
10	10.3111 in
11	11.0513 in
12	11.7500 in
13	12.4095 in
14	13.0319 in
15	13.6195 in
16	14.1740 in
17	14.6974 in
18	15.1915 in
19	15.6578 in
20	16.0980 in
21	16.5130 in

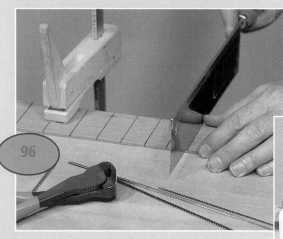

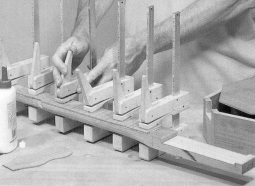

Step 14, 15 Saw slots for frets; trace outline of neck onto back of fretboard; glue and clamp fretboard to neck

Five-String Banjo Pattern Guide

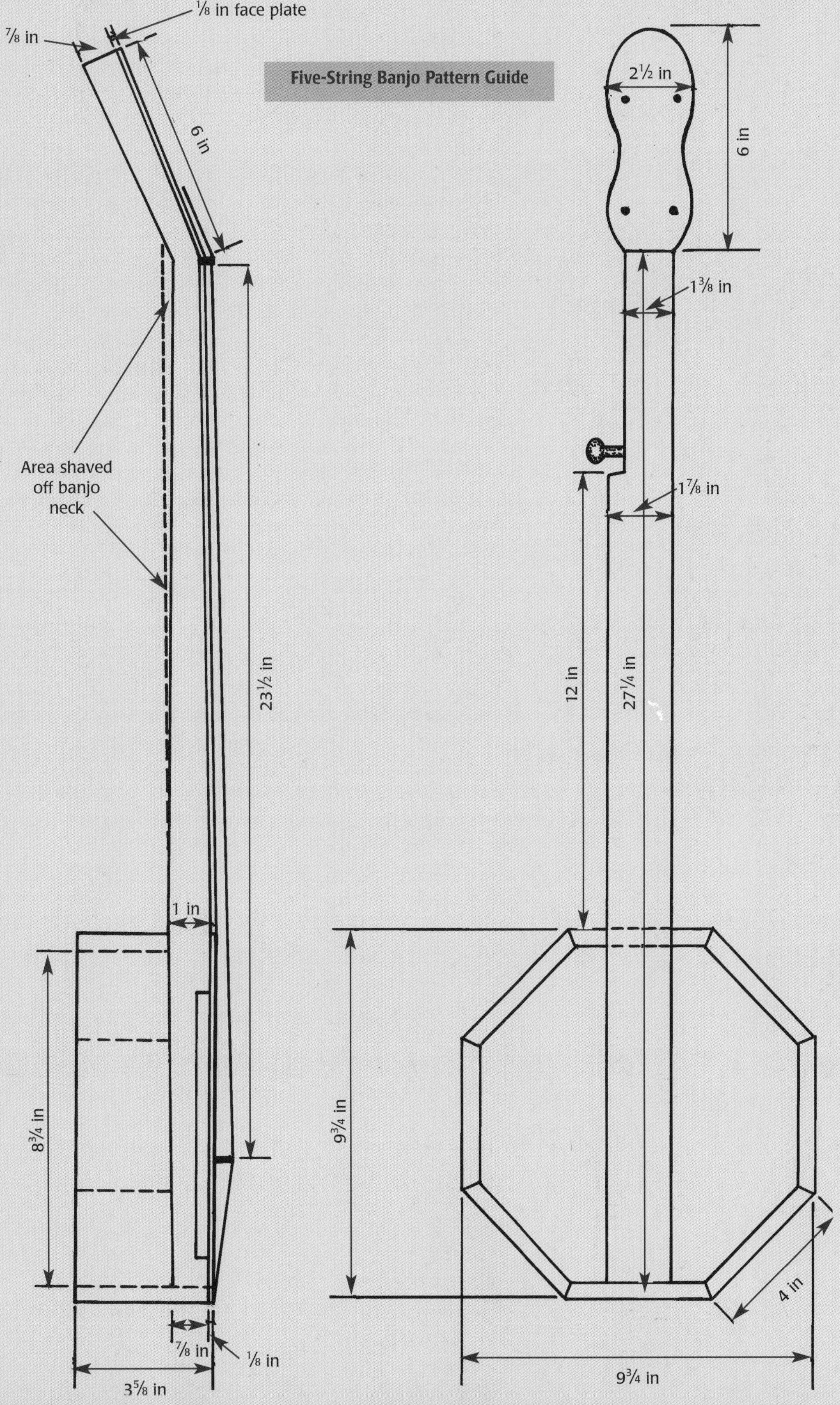

⅛ in face plate

⅞ in

6 in

Area shaved off banjo neck

23½ in

1 in

8¾ in

⅞ in

⅛ in

3⅝ in

2½ in

6 in

1⅜ in

1⅞ in

12 in

27¼ in

9¾ in

4 in

9¾ in

Step 17 Hammer frets into fretboard and dress the ends of the frets with a file

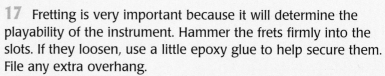

Step 18, 20 Drill hole for fifth peg; plot trajectory of strings from nut to bridge

Step 21 File the nut slots

17 Fretting is very important because it will determine the playability of the instrument. Hammer the frets firmly into the slots. If they loosen, use a little epoxy glue to help secure them. File any extra overhang.

Fifth Peg

18 The fifth peg will be installed into the side of the neck just behind the fifth fret. Measure fifth peg and drill a hole.

Setting the Action

19 The action is the distance of strings above frets dictated by the relationship of nut, neck angle, and bridge height. A proper string action makes the instrument easier to play. The neck should lay back a couple of degrees from being perfectly flat with the plane of the soundboard. This helps attain good string trajectory from nut to bridge and counteracts tendency of neck to pull forward under tension.

20 Mock up all components and, using a long ruler, plot the trajectory of the strings from nut to bridge. Make necessary adjustments to achieve good action. Study existing models.

Nut

21 Cut from bone, hardened plastic, or hardwood such as ebony. It should match width of fingerboard and fit in a slot at the fretboard/face plate juncture. Shape and glue in place. With a fine saw blade or knife-file (available at jeweler outlets) cut four slots into nut, as shown. Larger strings will require slightly larger slots. Cut them at a slight angle so they will slope from tuners and pass out of nut slot just barely ($1/32$ in) above fingerboard.

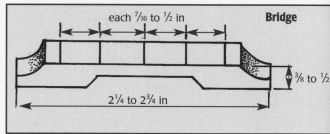

Nut

$1\,3/8$ in — each $3/8$ in — $1/8$ in — $1/8$ in — $1/4$

Bridge

22 Usually the height of the bridge will be

Bridge

each $7/16$ to $1/2$ in — $2\,1/4$ to $2\,3/4$ in — $3/8$ to $1/2$

between $3/8$ to $1/2$ in high and 2 to $2\,1/2$ in long. Draw bridge design onto a bridge blank and cut out. Cut fine shallow slots into the bridge at the prescribed points. Cut at a very slight angle to prevent strings from buzzing. **Option** Buy a ready-made bridge from a music store.

Assembly

23 Check fit of all parts before gluing. Beginning with neck/pot assembly, carefully glue and clamp all points of contact. Let dry. Glue and clamp the top to the pot.

24 After glue dries, trim off excess wood. Round all edges and sand smooth.

25 Finish using procedures suggested on p117.

Hitch Pins

26 Position five small pins to anchor strings at tail-end of banjo. Pre-drill, and hammer in. Use small finishing nails, piano bridge pins, or zither hitch pins.

Tuning Mechanisms

27 Disassemble the fifth peg and hammer it into the side of the neck, as shown. Place a small slot-head screw immediately in front of fifth peg on top of fingerboard to act as a tiny nut to guide the 5th string along the appropriate trajectory to the bridge.

28 Place tuners on peg head, pre-drill and attach securely with appropriate screws.

Strings

29 Use light- or medium-gauge, loop-end strings (found in sets for banjo at music stores). Before stringing up the instrument, find a small piece of leather or other resilient material to protect the area where the strings pass from hitch pins up-and-over the edge of the pot. Otherwise, strings will cut into wood at that point. Hook the loop to the hitch pin, pass the string up through the tuner hole and clip off excess string leaving 1 to 2 in of string to twist around peg.

Tuning

30 Follow common banjo tuning.

> 5th −E (highest note) −fifth string
> 4th −B (lowest note)
> 3rd −E (one octave lower than 5th string)
> 2nd −G#
> 1st −B

Playing the Five-String Banjo

If you have previous experience on a stringed instrument you may be able to explore the banjo fruitfully on your own. Sometimes a lesson from an experienced teacher is advisable.

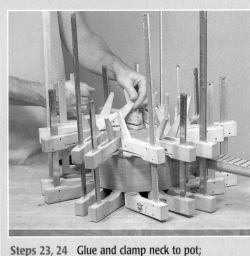

Steps 23, 24 Glue and clamp neck to pot; then soundboard to pot

Step 26 Drill holes for hitch pins

Step 27 Install fifth peg and tuning mechanisms to peg head; final stringing shows position of hitch pins, bridge, and protective leather piece on edge of soundboard

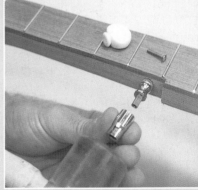

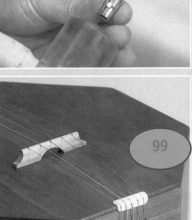

99

TEAR-DROP FIDDLE

The violin reached its highest level of perfection in the 16th, 17th, and 18th centuries in Cremona, Italy. Stradivarius, Amati, and Guarneri are accepted as the all-time master craftsmen of the violin who brought it to a standard of perfection that is still emulated and copied.

Before the advent of the violin, however, there were bowed instruments of every description in every corner of the world. Throughout history there have been experiments to vary the violin shape, size, and materials. During the 17th century, Savart experimented with a trapezoidal violin with some success. Examination of American folk culture reveals the cigar-box fiddle, spike fiddle, and beggar's fiddle. Though these instruments are not capable of the dynamic range of the classical violin, players nevertheless produce music of considerable delight. Today, however, the familiar shape of the classical violin has become the standard.

The fiddle in this project is reminiscent of fiddles found in Eastern Europe, the Middle East, and during the Medieval era in Western Europe. I've attempted to match its basic dimensions roughly to the measurements of a classical violin so that the player can switch from playing this fiddle to a more sophisticated violin.

Materials

Poster board
⅜ in plywood for back
⅛ in plywood for top (soundboard) and sides (ribs)
2 small maple end blocks
10 in x 2 in x 2 in maple block for neck
Tuning mechanisms
Violin fingerboard
Violin tailpiece, end pin, and tail gut
Violin bridge
Small piece of ebony or hardwood for nut and saddle
Softwood ¼ in dowel for soundpost
Strip of softwood for the bass bar
Set of standard violin strings
Violin bow (inexpensive)
Glue

Tools

Bandsaw, scroll saw, or coping saw
Hot pipe, bending iron, or steam cabinet for shaping ribs (sides)
Clamps
File and sandpaper
Drill and bit
Ruler
Chisel
Awl
Soundpost setting tool
Round tapered file
Finishing materials

Assembly

Pattern and Back

1 Draw full-size pattern (p103) of fiddle body on poster board. Cut out. Note Whatever the eventual shape, the width of instrument at bowing point should not exceed 5 in, so bow won't bump edge of sound box while bowing.

2 To make back, transfer body pattern onto ⅜ in plywood. Leave a little extra tongue at the neck end of pattern to fit heel of neck. Cut out back piece with bandsaw or coping saw, leaving a little extra margin around edges.

Ribs

3 Cut a strip 1⅜ in wide and 32 in long from ⅛ in plywood for the sides. A hot pipe, bending iron, or steam cabinet will probably be necessary to bend wood into conformation. The ribs of this fiddle are made from one continuous strip of wood. You may find it easier to make the ribs from two pieces which join at the tail end of the instrument.

Bending iron A more pronounced-shape standard violin is made using a bending iron (a hot pipe over which moistened wood is pressed and formed into various configurations). Professional bending irons feature a thermostat for heat regulation. Homemade bending irons may simply utilize a metal pipe and propane torch. Practice on a scrap of wood first.

Step 1 Create a template pattern. Trace pattern onto the wood stock for the back

Step 2 Cut out the back of the fiddle

Step 3 Bend ribs (sides) of fiddle on a bending iron

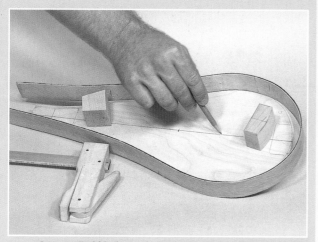

Step 4 End blocks ready for gluing; glue and clamp to back

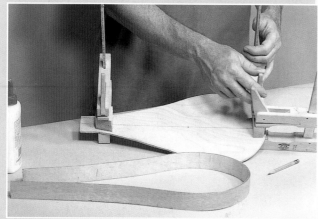

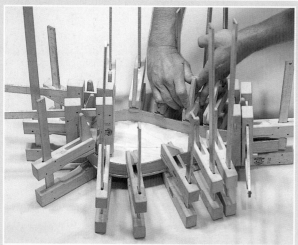

Step 7 Glue ribs to back

End Blocks

4 After shaping ribs, cut an end block from maple stock 1⅜ in high and 1½ in thick for neck joint. The exact shape of the ends of this block will be determined by the trajectory of the sides as they converge at the sound box/neck juncture. The width of the end block plus the ribs should be at least 1¼ in to accommodate a standard-size fingerboard.

5 At the tail end of the sound box, the end block should fit the curve formed by ribs and back. From maple, cut a 1⅜ in high, 2½ in wide, and 1 in thick end block. Sand and file so it conforms to tail-end curve. Prepare both end blocks for gluing.

6 Carefully center both blocks along a center line drawn on the inside of the back. Glue and clamp. Let dry.

Ribs to Back

7 Fit ribs to back/end blocks assembly. Glue and clamp.

8 When dry, file and sand all edges flush. Make sure everything is uniform height all around.

Neck and Peg Head

9 Draw pattern, as shown, onto top and side of a 10 in x 2 in x 2 in block of maple. If available, use a standard violin fingerboard to provide a pattern for the width and taper of the neck. If you use an alternative peg head design, make sure it accommodates the tuning mechanisms you've chosen.

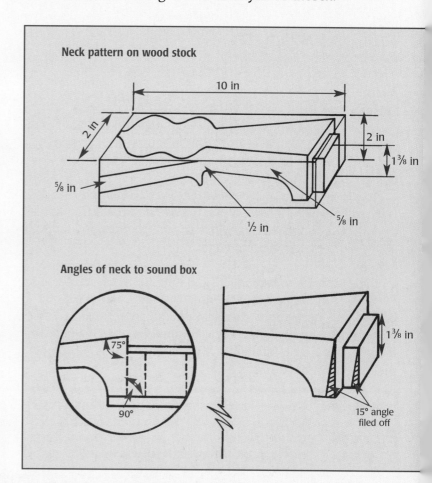

Neck pattern on wood stock

10 in
2 in
2 in
1⅜ in
⅝ in
½ in
⅝ in

Angles of neck to sound box

75°
90°
15° angle filed off
1⅜ in

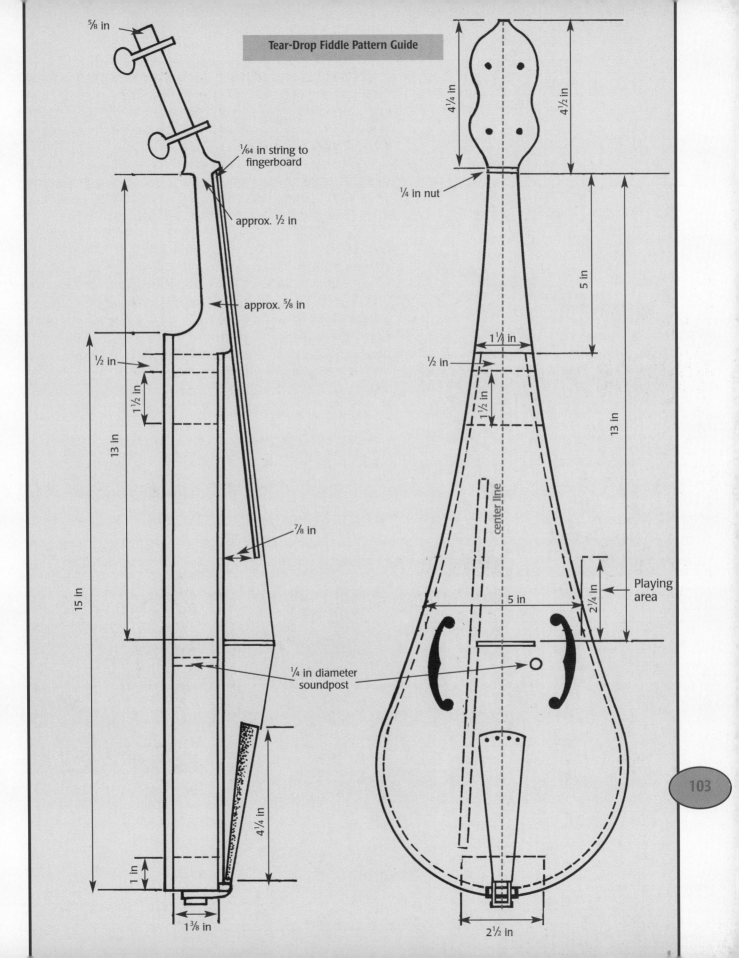

Tear-Drop Fiddle Pattern Guide

⁵⁄₈ in

¹⁄₆₄ in string to fingerboard

approx. ½ in

approx. ⁵⁄₈ in

½ in

1½ in

13 in

15 in

⁷⁄₈ in

¼ in diameter soundpost

4¼ in

1 in

1³⁄₈ in

4¼ in

4½ in

¼ in nut

5 in

1¼ in

½ in

1½ in

13 in

center line

5 in

2¼ in

Playing area

2½ in

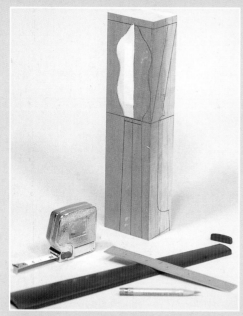

Step 9, 10 Trace neck and peg head pattern onto neck blank; saw out the neck

10 Use a bandsaw to cut out the basic form.
11 After all cuts have been completed, round the underside of neck and peg head with files, as shown.
12 Calculate the placement of your chosen tuning mechanisms and drill holes with an appropriate-size drill bit, as shown.

Fitting Neck to Sound Box

13 Measure and mark a center line the length of the instrument to insure correct alignment of neck to sound box. Be sure that when neck is butted to center of upper end block, everything lines up perfectly with center line, see pattern, p103.
14 Cut and file the heel end of neck at a 15° incline relative to the end block, see p102, so neck will lay back a little. This insures a string trajectory necessary for good action (proper relationship between nut, fingerboard, and bridge necessary for easy playing).
15 Finish the neck-to-sound-box junction, as shown. This is an effective kind of mortise and tenon joint, using the ribs to form a notch (the mortise) into which the neck tenon fits. Take time to carefully saw, chisel, and file until all aspects of the heel of the neck fit perfectly to the sound box.

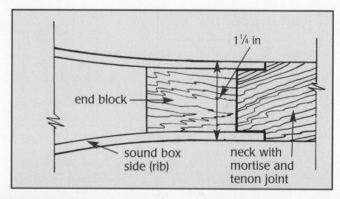

Step 11 Shape and smooth neck with files

Step 12 Drill holes for tuning mechanisms

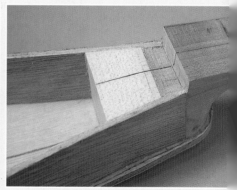

Step 15 Fit neck to sound box; detail of neck mortise and tenon joint

Soundboard

16 Trace the actual sound box shape onto a piece of ⅛ in plywood. Cut with a saw, leaving a little margin for error.

Sound Holes

17 I have chosen an historical sound hole design from the European Renaissance. You can choose your own design but it must be large enough and located so that the soundpost–which fits close to the foot on the treble side of the bridge–can be inserted and accessed for positioning with a soundpost setting tool (see steps 20 and 28). Trace the sound hole patterns onto the soundboard (see patterns, p120) and saw them out with a scroll saw. File and sand to uniformity.

Fingerboard

18 If this is your first fiddle project, I suggest buying an inexpensive stock fingerboard, tailpiece, end pin, tail gut (connects the tailpiece to the end pin), and bridge since these are fairly difficult items for the novice maker. They can be found in any violin repair shop or you can send to a company specializing in string instrument products.

Mock-up

19 Fit neck to sound box, clamp fingerboard to neck, and place soundboard on top of sound box, all without glue. Measure the distance from the top surface of the end of the fingerboard to the top surface of the sound box. It should be within ¹⁄₁₆ in either side of ⅞ in. If your measurements are not true, make adjustments in the heel of the neck at the mortise and tenon joint. Be sure the base of the heel fits flat to the back heel tab. There are no shortcuts to fitting these crucial elements. Time and careful handwork will eventually do the job.

Bridge Placement

20 While the soundboard and fingerboard are in position, mark the placement of the bridge by measuring 13 in from the nut. The distance from the end of the fingerboard to bridge should be 2¼ in.

Bass Bar

21 The bass bar is designed to provide strength to the violin top and reinforce and transmit the frequencies of the low strings the full length of the soundboard. Cut this bar from a strip of stiff softwood. The bass bar is positioned directly under the left foot of the bridge on the low-string side. It angles slightly, moving towards the center line at the neck end. Glue the bass bar in place.

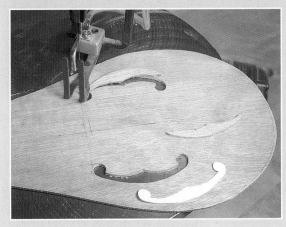

Step 17 Saw sound holes with a scroll saw

Step 18 Measure height of fingerboard to soundboard

Step 21 Glue and clamp the bass bar to the inside of the soundboard

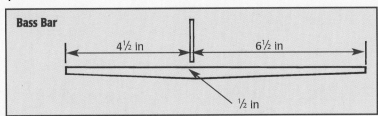

Bass Bar

4½ in   6½ in

½ in

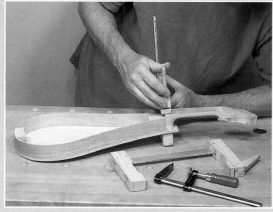

Step 22   Glue neck to sound box

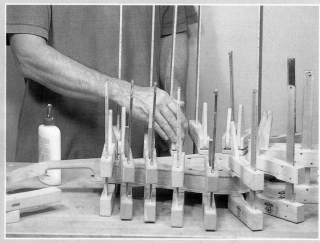

Step 23   Glue soundboard to sound box

Step 24   Drill end pin hole

Step 25   Glue fingerboard to neck; ready for final "fitting up"

Neck to Sound Box

22   After you are satisfied with the neck/sound box fit and checked its alignment to center line and other measurement guidelines, glue and clamp neck to sound box. Let dry.

Soundboard to Sound Box

23   Fit and glue the soundboard carefully in place. Let dry. File and sand all edges.

End Pin

24   Drill a hole through the end block to receive the end pin and gradually enlarge it with a round tapered file or a peg-hole reamer until the end pin fits tightly. Do not glue in place. It should be a friction fit. You will use this hole later as a peep hole for helping line up the soundpost.

Fingerboard and Nut

25   Buy or make a nut from ebony or other hardwood. Glue the fingerboard and nut onto the neck. Grooves cut into the nut should be $7/32$ in apart and deep enough so that the distance between the bottom of the string to the fingerboard is $1/64$ in.

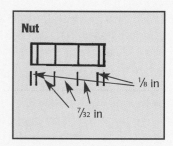

Nut

$1/8$ in

$7/32$ in

Saddle

26   Chisel a small notch at the end of the sound box to receive a small piece of ebony or hardwood called a saddle. This prevents the tailpiece gut from cutting into the edge of the top.

Finishing

27   Sand carefully and finish the instrument (see p117). The top of the fingerboard is left unfinished.

Soundpost

28   The soundpost, made from a length of $1/4$ in straight-grained spruce, is lightly wedged between the top and the back of the fiddle for two reasons: 1) to enhance the overall dynamic response of the instrument by setting the back into vibration, and 2) to help support the top

which is under great pressure when the strings are at full tension. The approximate length of the soundpost can be judged by inserting it into the instrument through the sound hole and marking the length required. With the help of a soundpost setter, insert the post into the instrument, set the post upright about ⅛ in below the right foot of the bridge. Install carefully. Viewing through the end pin hole will help in getting it vertically aligned. Several adjustments may be needed to make it fit properly.

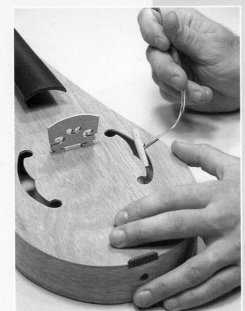

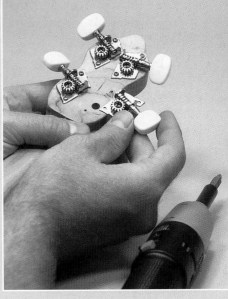

Installing Tuners

29 Put tuners in place and mark the screw holes with an awl. Select a drill bit that is slightly smaller than the screws provided and pre-drill the holes. Carefully screw on the tuners.

Step 26, 29 Set-up the soundpost; install tuning mechanisms

Tail Gut

30 Install the end pin. Adjust the tail gut so the end of tailpiece is as close as possible to bottom edge of instrument.

Stringing

31 Buy a standard set of violin strings. Insert each string end into the tailpiece and wrap other end of each string around its respective tuning peg. Take up the slack and set the bridge into position.

Step 30, 31 Install saddle and tailpiece with tailpiece gut; peg head stringing arrangement

Tuning the Fiddle

32 The second string from the highest is tuned to concert pitch which is called A-440 (a string vibrating 440 times per second will produce the pitch of A). The third string or next lowest is then tuned a D. The lowest string is a G and the highest string is tuned to E. On the first tuning or when changing strings, several rounds of tuning are usually necessary because the strings stretch and new instruments take time to settle under tension. Reset the bridge to vertical as you bring the strings up to pitch, since It usually moves as the strings are tightened.

Bows

33 Buy an inexpensive bow. If you make your own, use horse hair, available through a supply house or your local violin repairman.

Playing Suggestions

You might also consider using a standard violin chin rest and shoulder rest if you plan to play the instrument under your chin. Traditionally, fiddle players hold the instrument down on their arm as they fiddle away.

107

CELTIC HARP

Early Sumerian and Egyptian harps and the Greek lyre were popular chordophones in ancient times. Today, the harp, in all its many manifestations, remains among the most venerable of all stringed instruments.

The familiar triangular-shaped harp was probably developed in Scotland during the 8th and 9th centuries. By the mid to late 15th century, the Scottish and Irish clarsach became a standard form. In Europe, the harp was held in highest esteem until the 16th century when the lute and keyboard families gained in popularity.

Throughout its European history, the harp evolved through many variations in shape and size from oversize to small and portable, from as few as seven strings, to forty or more.

The oldest extant harps are found in Ireland and Scotland and date from the 15th century. Harps of this vintage were wire strung with sound boxes beautifully carved from a solid block of wood. By the 18th century, harps switched from wire strings to gut strings to accommodate the stylistic changes occurring in the music. Today, the vogue is for hand-made, nylon-strung Celtic harps, which come in a dazzling variety of old and new styles and sizes. This project is a small, nylon-strung instrument based on traditional Irish (or Celtic) harp style.

Materials

Poster board
¼ in sheet of quality plywood or solid wood for
   sound box
6 ft x 6 in x 1 in thick maple hardwood for end blocks,
   neck, forepillar, base plate (optional)
2–26 in x ¾ in x ⅛ in thick maple hardwood strips
   for string ribs
2⅜ in x ¼ in lengths of hardwood for sound box
   linings
2 lag bolts
Harp string grommets
Nylon strings (for gauges, see chart, p116)
Zither pins (or tapered pins) and tuning wrench
Glue

Tools

Bandsaw, handsaw, jigsaw
Plane and sander
Files and chisel
Reamer
Drill and appropriate bits
Clamps
Awl
Finishing materials

Assembly

Full-Size Pattern

1 On a large piece of poster board or heavy paper make a full-size side view and front view drawing of harp from pattern, pp111 and 113. The success of your instrument rests largely on the accuracy of this master drawing. Cut out the parts to use as templates.

Sound Box Components

2 The main sound box components (back, sides, and soundboard) may be constructed from either ¼ in plywood or solid hardwood stock resawn to ¼ in thickness. Using the templates, transfer the measurements, as shown, to plywood sheet. Cut out components, leaving a little extra margin for fitting later.

End Blocks

3 Use 1 in hardwood to make lower end block 9 in x 6 in x 1 in and upper block 4 in x 2½ in x 1 in. The front or soundboard side of lower and upper end blocks is beveled to accommodate tapered shape of sound box, as defined by the side pieces. Begin assembling the sound box by gluing the sides to the two end blocks.

Back

4 Cut holes in back to access sound box interior for stringing purposes. The proportion and spacing of these access holes are variable although it is helpful if they approximate hand-size and are positioned so that all interior string holes can be accessed from outside the harp.

Harp Soundboards

The soundboard is the most vulnerable part of a harp since it has to support hundreds of pounds of string tension. It must be strong but flexible. In spite of the number of strings, string material (steel, brass, bronze, nylon, gut, etc.), size of harp, type of music, etc., most anything will work if the construction is solid.

Better grade multiple plys of hardwoods give more strength. Sitka spruce plywood, available from harp mail order shops, is the first choice. These high-grade speciality plywoods are best for tone and strength to weight ratio. However, quality store-bought plywoods, if well prepared and not overly taxed, are adequate for a good sounding harp.

Both solid hardwood and softwood soundboards are used by more exclusive harp makers since they provide the best sound. These are harder to prepare, however, and more susceptible to cracking. Work carefully and slowly for best results.

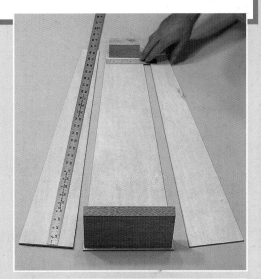

Steps 1, 2
Make full-size pattern templates; sound box components

Step 4
Rough drill access holes into back

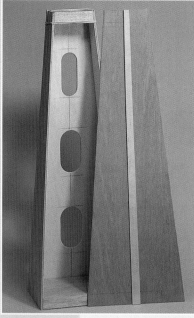

Step 6 Glue and clamp string rib to soundboard

Step 7 Sound box assembly, note access holes in back

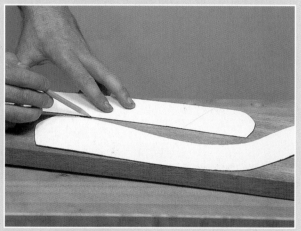

Step 8 Transfer neck and pillar pattern to wood; saw out neck on bandsaw

110

Soundboard

5 Most soundboards are about ¼ in thick and are usually graduated from thicker in the low string range to thinner toward the high range. I glued two ⅛ in pieces of plywood together, cut the soundboard pattern out, then thinned it on the inside face with planes and a sander.

String Rib

6 Two hardwood strips called string ribs, measuring the length of the soundboard and about ⅛ in thick (¾ in wide at the bottom with a taper to ½ in at the top) support the soundboard when under tension. (Laminated soundboards on smaller harps usually only require an inner string rib.) Draw the string rib pattern, p111, twice onto an appropriate stick of hardwood (maple) and cut out two strips on bandsaw. Taper, shape, sand, and glue one of the string ribs to the outside of the soundboard, exactly along its center line, as shown. Use enough clamps to achieve even pressure all along the full length.

7 The inner reinforcing string rib, approximately 2 in shorter than the outer string rib, fits between the end blocks and is now glued to the inside of the soundboard to provide more stability against the great pull of the strings. Set the sound box assembly, back, and soundboard aside.

Neck and Forepillar

8 Make the neck and forepillar template patterns from your full-size drawing, cut out, and place them on a 1-in-thick plank of hardwood (maple, high-grade mahogany, walnut, or cherry). Trace outlines onto the wood and cut them out on the bandsaw leaving a little extra wood at all joining points.

9 Begin a rough fitting of all parts. Prepare the lap joint at the neck/pillar junction. Mark and cut the lap joint, according to drawing. Now adjust the three primary components so there is a reasonable fit of the neck and forepillar to the sound box. Use planes, files, chisel, and sanding devices to accomplish this. Proceed from step to step, true up each part a little at a time, and refine as you go.

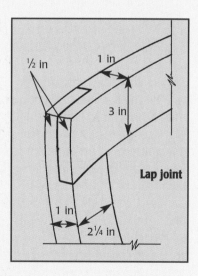

½ in   1 in

3 in

Lap joint

1 in

2¼ in

Soundboard String Holes

10 After the first fitting of the three major components, plot the sequence of eighteen string holes along the soundboard string rib.

Step 8 Cut neck/forepillar lap joint; lap joint detail
Step 9 Rough fit of all parts

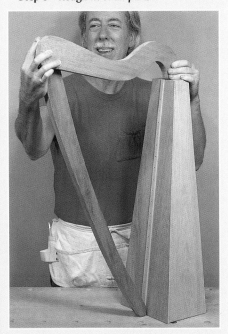

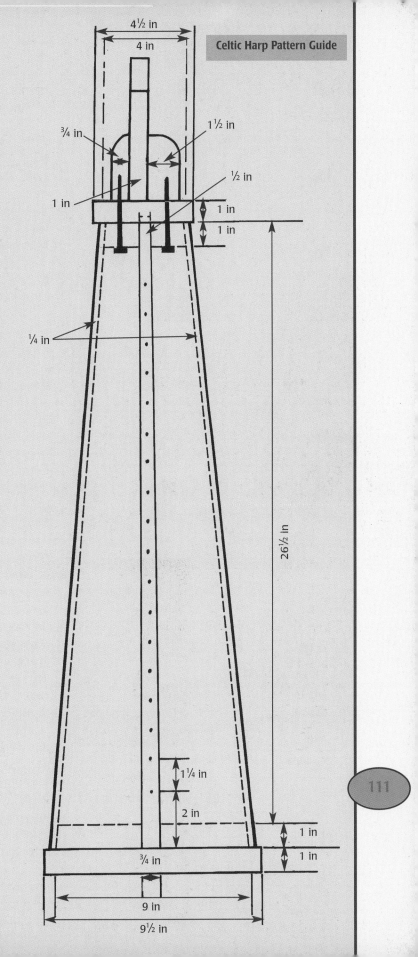

4½ in

4 in

¾ in

1½ in

½ in

1 in

1 in

1 in

¼ in

26½ in

1¼ in

2 in

1 in

1 in

¾ in

9 in

9½ in

Step 11
Carefully plot
the string
holes and
drill holes in
string rib

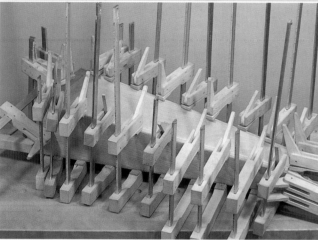

Step 12   Glue and clamp soundboard to sound box

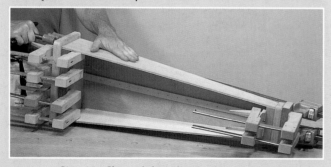

Step 14   Glue and clamp base and cap to sound box

Step 16
Chisel small
notch in pillar
foot to fit
string rib

Beginning at the bass end, mark the placement of the lowest string leaving at least a 1 in margin from where the foot of the pillar meets the sound box. Chart the holes equidistant along the string rib at 1¼ in intervals.

11　You have the option of drilling different-size holes in the string rib relative to the diameter of the strings themselves: bass strings require larger holes than the smaller-diameter high strings. Reinforce each string hole with a grommet so that when strings are tensioned they will not cut into wood. Various sizes of specialty harp grommets are available. Drill holes into the string rib so that the grommets fit snugly.

Soundboard Linings

12　Linings provide more gluing surface for the soundboard. Cut thin strips of hardwood into ⅜ in x ¼ in lengths to fit along length of interior sides of sound box. Glue the linings in place. When dry, sand everything uniform and fit soundboard to sound box frame until there is good contact all around. Glue and clamp the soundboard to sound box, as shown.

Base (optional)

13　This is an optional base for the bottom of the sound box. The design of the base will help balance the harp so it will stand on its own and also add a finished look to bottom of instrument. To add a base, glue a slightly outsize plate of 1 in maple to the bottom of the sound box. Later, to finish base, add two small feet so harp stands securely and balances without tipping over.

Sound Box Cap

14　Cut and adjust thickness of sound box cap that fits between neck and top of sound box. By adjusting thickness of cap, you can help bring all the components into better conformation. Like the sound box base, the cap helps dress up the top of the sound box. Proceed with final adjustments between cap, sound box, neck, and forepillar, shimming or trimming as required. Glue the cap to the top of sound box.

Mock-up

15　At this point, mock-up all components. Temporarily clamp neck and forepillar together and set this assembly slightly off from center in relation to the center line of the sound box to allow the strings a more vertical alignment to the string rib. Calculate the exact placement of the neck shoulder on the sound box cap. Do the same with the foot of the forepillar where it joins the sound box. Cut a small notch into the foot of pillar to accommodate string rib. (Alternatively, the string rib could be shortened to accommodate the pillar foot.) As you proceed, continue to true up any misfitting joints.

16　The shoulder or neck knob at the neck/sound box juncture is now buttressed with extra wood creating extra stability by generating more gluing area. Laminate small

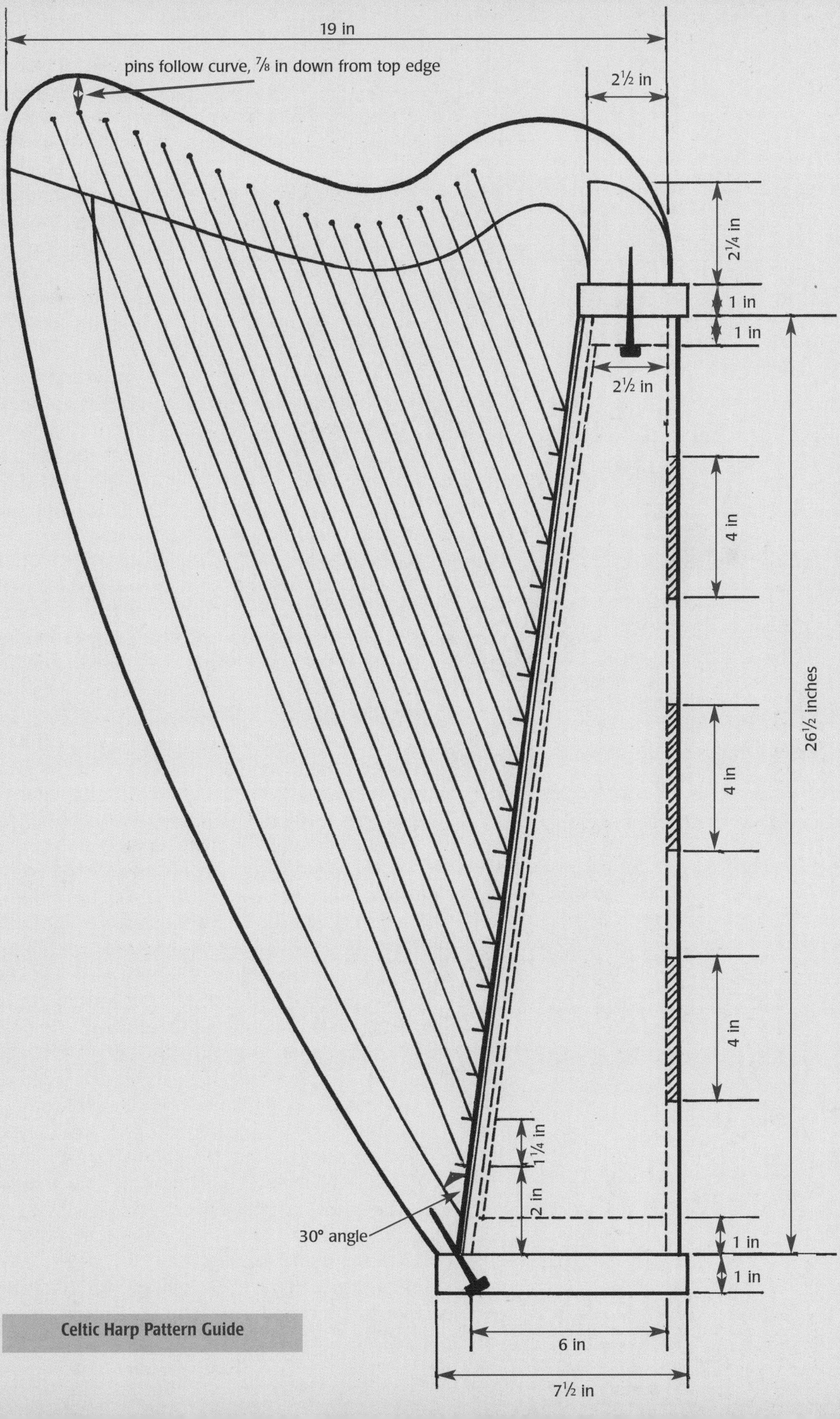

19 in

pins follow curve, 7/8 in down from top edge

2 1/2 in

2 1/4 in

1 in

1 in

2 1/2 in

4 in

4 in

26 1/2 inches

4 in

1 1/4 in

2 in

30° angle

1 in

1 in

6 in

7 1/2 in

Celtic Harp Pattern Guide

113

Step 16 Buttress shoulder of neck; glue and clamp wood to neck shoulder

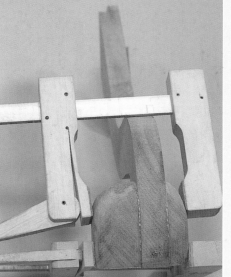

Step 19 Drill holes for tuning pins

Step 20 Round all edges and sand the various components

blocks of wood on both sides (less on right side than left since the neck is off-set) and shape, as shown. (Examine existing harps for more elaborate modeling of this site.)

Tuning Pin Information

17 Zither pins or tapered pins are used on most Celtic harps today. Zither pins will be drilled into the left side of the neck relative to the player. Note Tapered pins, which pass all the way through the neck, are more difficult to find but in the long run, probably provide better service. The large ends of the tapered pins are milled to accommodate matching tuning wrenches. Since there are varying standards, buy the tuning wrench at the same time as the tapered pins. A small hole is drilled into the opposite end to receive the string. The tapered pin holes are first drilled all the way through the neck with a regular small bit, then enlarged to a taper (working from right to left relative to the player) with a reamer that matches the taper of the pins.

Pin Placement on the Neck

18 Spacing of tuning pins will be variable due to the changing contour of the neck. On the side view of your master drawing, see pattern, p113, plot the tuning pin positions along the neck using the following procedure. First, locate the position of the longest string between the string rib and the neck. Connect these two points. Now draw a line perpendicular to the bass string. Along this line, mark ⅝ in increments. Now derive the pattern of hole spacing along the neck by drawing lines between the string rib hole positions and points along the perpendicular line. All string lines should be parallel to the first bass string. Make any adjustments necessary to achieve a reasonable configuration.

19 Pin positions should follow the contour of the top of the neck and about ⅞ in away, see pattern, p113. Transfer the measurements from the template drawing to the actual neck using an awl to mark the tuning pin positions. Double check all measurements. Finally, drill holes at the designated points that will receive the zither or tapered tuning pins.

Last Fitting and Assembly

20 After rounding all edges and sanding the various components, it is now time to glue the neck and forepillar together at the lap joint.

21 From the inside of the sound box, drill two holes through the upper end block and sound box cap into the shoulder of the neck to receive two lag bolts, which will secure this important joint. Note that the lag bolts should pass freely through the end block and cap, but screw securely into the shoulder of the neck, so that when the bolt is tightened the neck is pulled flush to the cap and end block. This will require two sizes of drill bits.

22 After one last fitting, drill a hole through the base of the sound box and into the foot of the pillar. Without gluing, screw the entire assembly together and make any necessary adjustments so that all parts fit snugly.

Gluing

23 Finally, apply glue to all contact points on sound box, pillar, and neck. Assemble and screw in all lag bolts. With lag bolts, there is no need to clamp. Check all joints for alignment. Let dry completely.

Note   Many harp makers prefer to leave these junctures unglued in the event the harp needs repair as it adjusts and shifts under applied string tension.

24 Glue the back to the sound box.

25 Add optional feet to bottom of instrument.

Clean-up and Preparation for Finishing

26 Clean up all glue drips and smears with a chisel, sandpaper, and a damp rag. Trim all excess overhang of the soundboard and back from around the sound box. Round all edges and corners to give the harp a smooth and soft impression. Time taken here will greatly increase the final appearance and beauty of the instrument.

Step 20   Drill holes for neck/sound box lag bolts

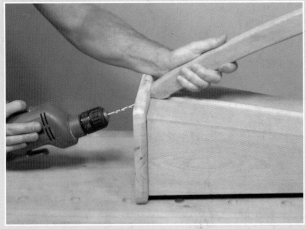

Step 22   Final fitting and assembly without glue; drill hole in base/pillar foot juncture for lag bolt

Steps 24, 25   Detail of feet on base of harp; glue back to sound box

Steps 29, 31   String and tune

Harp String Gauge Chart

String #	Note	Gauge
1 (Short)	D	.025
2	C	.025
3	B	.025
4	A	.025
5	G	.028
6	F	.028
7	E	.028
8	D	.032
9	C	.032
10	B	.036
11	A	.036
12	G	.040
13	F	.040
14	E	.045
15	D	.045
16 (Middle C)	C	.050
17	B	.050
18 (long)	A	.055

Total tension: 433 lbs

Decoration

27 Decorate at this time, if desired. Use wood burning techniques, painting, or carving to enhance the appearance of the harp.

Finishing

28 Proceed through the finishing stages (p117).

Fitting and Stringing

29 Install chosen tuning mechanisms. Insert string-rib grommets. See diagram below for tying the specialized string knot required at the sound box. Secure each string to its respective tuning device. Gradually bring up the pitch. Don't worry about tuning the strings to final pitch yet since pitch stability will be achieved only after many sessions over a period of time. As part of this adjustment, the soundboard will take on a characteristic belly or curve as a result of the string tension. This is desirable and makes the soundboard act somewhat like a tightened drum head.

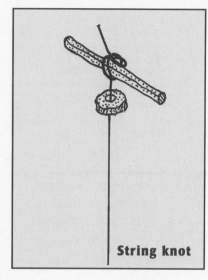

String knot

30 If for any reason some anomaly occurs while stringing-up, analyze the situation, sleep on it, then deal with it. You know your instrument better than anybody and by this time you can make any adjustments necessary.

Tuning

31 The harp will tune to approximately a C or D diatonic scale spanning two octaves and a fourth. Work from extremes of string range in towards the middle, pulling the strings gradually closer to their final pitch levels. A pitch pipe or electronic tuner will aid you in this process.

Playing the Celtic Harp

The harp is exclusively a plucked chordophone, but within this realm is capable of formulating melody, harmony, and rhythm in varying ways. Generally, the harp is played modally: major and minor modes are created depending on the note you wish to call "do."

Many professional harps are fitted with semitone levers (mechanisms added to the harp for changing the pitch ½ chromatic step). Another refinement includes bridge pins (small unthreaded pins with a notch towards the end) that are positioned just under each tuning pin. These help guide all the strings to a consistent plane across the playing area.

The serious luthier will spend as much time on the finishing stages of the instrument as on the actual making. With the development of modern finishing products, however, the length of time can be shortened considerably.

Varnish

This finish provides a hard surface and offers good protection from the elements. Oil-base varnishes were traditionally used for fine violins during the 1700s. The quality of this finish is certainly unquestionable, but its extremely long drying time makes its use impractical for the amateur maker. Spirit-based varnishes, (those that use paint thinner, mineral spirits, or turpentine as a base), provide a good hard protective finish and have a much shorter drying time. These varnishes are often designated as interior or furniture varnishes. Spar varnish is not recommended for instruments. Plastic varnishes can be useful for finishing many instruments, although their use is not recommended for finer instruments because of the possible effects the plastic may have on the sound quality. Water-based varnishes are easy to use and have the advantage of drying quickly and providing an easy-care surface. Usually two or three light coats of the chosen varnish are sufficient to provide protection for your instrument. Most finishes come in high gloss, semi-gloss, matt, or flat types of luster. The choice depends on personal taste.

Oil

This finish is preferred by many fine woodworking artists because it seals, conditions, and protects all at once. Danish, linseed, Swedish, and tung oils are a few of the oils available. Most of these oils are waterproof and dry to a hard finish. Oils are easy to apply and with a bit of polishing they yield a lustrous finish. Plastic oils are also available but their use for fine musical instruments is limited. Since different oils have different application requirements be sure to follow the directions on the container and talk to a knowledgeable person about the different brands available. Two to four coats of oil are usually sufficient for a good finish depending on the hardness of the wood.

Shellac

Shellac gives an especially fine finish when used with French polishing techniques. Its main detraction, however, is that it is not impervious to liquids. I find that shellac is most beneficial when used as a sealer applied under varnish. It is a natural product and soaks into the wood and dries hard. Shellac is thinned with methyl hydrate. White shellac is recommended rather than orange shellac.

Lacquer

Lacquer is favored by modern luthiers because it dries quickly and provides a very hard finish. It is usually sprayed on with a compressed or airless spray gun or comes in a compressed can. Brushing is possible but difficult. Though relatively expensive it is the quickest finish for a short-term project. Several thin coats of lacquer produce a finish that is impervious to almost everything. A sanding sealer is recommended for a sealing coat under the lacquer. Three or four light coats give the best results.

Stains

The application of a stain is optional. Stains are usually used to add warmth and color to wood and to enhance the grain. Proper staining is an art that requires some patience and experimentation. Liquid or gelled ready-to-use stains are the easiest to use. Walnut or mahogany are good basic shades that you might consider. There are also water-based, alcohol-based, and oil-based stains (some of which use aniline dyes), each with its own unique qualities.

FINISHING PROCEDURES

Sanding

1 Sand the instrument with number 120 sandpaper to remove all glue smudges and uneven surfaces.
2 Sand again with number 220 sandpaper in order to achieve a perfectly smooth surface. Your fingers can tell when the wood is beginning to be polished.
3 Finer grades of sandpaper may be used for an additional polish.

Stain

4 Stain is optional. Experiment on a scrap of wood before applying the stain to your instrument. Follow the directions on the container. If you rub the surface with number 000 steel wool after it has been stained and dried, this will lighten and highlight the finish.

Sealing

5 A sealing coat may be applied before or after the stain depending on how dark you want the stain to color. Stain first before sealing for a dark color; seal first and then stain if you want the stain to take lightly. Some stains have sealing elements already in them so you can accomplish two steps at once.

Top Coats

6 After a light rubbing with fine steel wool on the stained and sealed surface, dust with a soft clean rag. Find a dust free environment in which to apply the protective coats.

7 The first coat should be the lightest or thinned the most (with the exception of oil finishes) and each successive coat should be slightly heavier.
8 Rub the surface with 000 steel wool or very fine sandpaper between each coat of finish to remove imperfections and drips and to smooth the surface in preparation for the next coat. Dust well and repeat the application.

Polish

9 After the last coat of finish has been applied, rub the surface lightly with fine steel wool and polish with a soft cloth to highlight the finish. A higher gloss may be achieved with the use of a pumice stone polishing aid used with oil or water and buffed to a high sheen.

Wax

10 Finally, a paste or liquid wax (carnauba wax) or specialty instrument waxes can be applied to give extra protection.

The tools you use to make your instrument must be sharp. Dull tools are a source of danger and frustration.

Traditionally, sharpening was done on whet stones using oil or water as a lubricant. The process began with the use of a grinding stone or very coarse stone and progressed to a hard smooth stone. The honing was usually done freehand, allowing experience and feel to guide the blade to produce just the right bevel on the cutting edge. Stones still give a superior cutting edge and the invention of honing guides has made it much easier to get a uniform bevel and shaving edge.

Stones come in a variety of sizes and shapes depending on the size and shape of the blade being sharpened. Some stones are available in combinations, a different grade on each side. A grinding stone is usually necessary to sharpen tools that have been badly damaged or abused or to prepare new blades that are unsharpened. A course carborundum stone is often used for blades that have minor chips or are very dull. The India stone, which comes in a medium and fine grit, is an intermediary honing stone used to prepare the blade for a fine stone. A Washita stone is a good basic stone for medium to fine honing as is the soft Arkansas stone. A hard Arkansas stone is usually used to produce a fine shaving edge on the tool and the leather strop to remove the metal burr or wire and put a final polish on the blade. All stones are used with a medium to light grade honing oil. At its most basic, sharpening jobs require two stones—medium and fine. Synthetic stones are also available.

Sandpaper and emery cloth have also been used effectively for sharpening. A power sander may be used for the initial grinding stages followed by progressively finer grades of sandpaper and finally a fine emery cloth. It is possible to produce a shaving edge by this method. Sandpaper and emery cloth also have the advantage of being very inexpensive and easy to find.

SHARPENING PROCEDURE

The blade may need to be ground on a grinding wheel, belt sander, or coarse stone depending on its condition. Do not leave the blade on a power grinder long enough for it to change color because it will lose its temper and quickly dull again. Cool it in water often as you grind.

Hone the blade at a slightly increased angle (½ to

1°) on a medium stone (India, Washita, or soft Arkansas) until an even polished bevel has been achieved across the blade. A honing guide will help you hold a consistent angle and aid in controlling the pressure. Note that the underside of the blade should be flat across its entire width. Lay the blade flat or at a slightly increased angle on its back and grind away until you achieve a flat surface across its width.

On a fine stone (hard Arkansas) at the same angle or slightly increased by one-half degree, hone the blade to a high polish. Take time to do this carefully.

To remove the hair edge or burr that will probably develop, pull the blade along a leather strop quickly with good pressure on both sides. This will produce a final polished shaving edge.

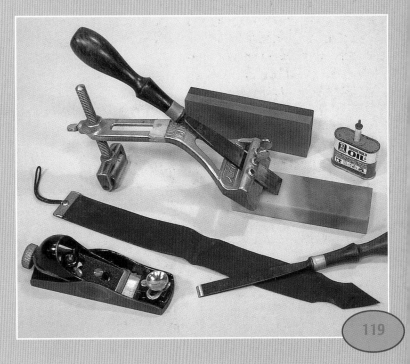

SOUND HOLE SUGGESTIONS

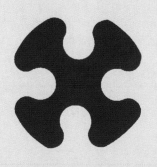

Celtic harp

Starburst

Cloverleaf

"f"-hole

Renaissance style

Weeping heart

Crescent

Reference Books and Periodicals for Instrument Making

The following references have been selected because they are applicable to the contents of this book. No listings for the guitar have been included because that instrument is beyond the scope of this material. If you wish more extensive listings consult *The Folk Music Sourcebook* published by Oak Publications, 33 West 60th St., NY, NY 10023.

Instrument-Making Needs

All companies listed below provide interesting catalogues for a nominal fee. Ask for an up-to-date price list.

Albert Constantine and Son Inc., 2050 Eastchester Road, Bronx, NY 10461 Complete line of luthier tools, books, and materials

Bill Lewis, 3607 W. Broadway, Vancouver, BC V6R 2B8. Educational catalogue listing a well researched variety of tools and accessories.

H.L. Wild, 510 E. 11th St., NY, NY 10009

International Violin Supply Co., 414 East Baltimore St., Baltimore, Md 21202. Stringed instrument necessities.

Joseph F. Wallo, 1319 F St. Northwest, Washington D.C. 20004. General selection for all the maker's needs.

Marina Music, 1892 Union St., San Francisco, CA 94123. Wood, accessories, and tools.

Vitali Import Col., 5944 Atlantic Blvd., Maywood, CA 90270. Tools, accessories, and materials for the specialist.

Craftswoods, 5908C Macleod Tr. S., Calgary, Alberta T2H 0K1. All the woods you can't find any place else. Exotica.

Making and Repairing Instruments

How to Make a Banjo and a Banjo Guitar, G.W. Stamm, Stamm Industries, 813 W. Lovell St., Kalamazoo, Mich 49007

Classic Guitar Construction, Irvine Sloane, E.P. Dutton and Co., Inc., NY, NY

Guitar Repair, Irvine Sloane, E.P. Dutton and Co., Inc., NY, NY

Classic Guitar Making, Arthur E. Overholtzer, Brock Pub. Col, P.O. Box 40430, San Francisco, CA

Violin Making As It Was and Is, Heron-Allen, Ward Lock Limited, 116 Baker St., London, England

Complete Guitar Repair, Hideo Kamimoto, Oak Publications, 33 W. 60th St., NY, NY 10023

SUGGESTED READING

How To Make and Play the Dulcimore, Chet Hines, Stackpole Books, Cameron and Kelker Streets, Harrisburg, PA 17105

Making A Simple Violin and Viola, Ronald Roberts, David and Charles Inc., North Pomfret, VT 05053

The Classical Guitar, McLeod and Welford, The Dryad Press, Wood-Ridge, NJ 07075

Drums, Tomtoms, and Rattles, Bernard Mason, Dover Pub., Inc., 180 Varick St., NY, NY 10014

Country Instruments, Makin' Your Own, Andy dePaule, Oliver Press, 1400 Ryan Creek Rd., Willits, CA 95490

Making and Playing Bamboo Pipes, Margaret Galloway, The Dryad Press, Wood-Ridge, NJ 07075

The Violin Maker's Guide, H.E. Brown, International Guitar and Import Co., Tulsa, Oklahoma

The Amateur Wind Instrument Maker, Trevor Robinson, University of Massachusetts Press, Amherst, MA 01002

Musical Instruments Made To Be Played, Ronald Roberts, The Dryad Press, Wood-Ridge, NJ 07075

Constructing the Mountain Dulcimer, Dean Kimball, David McKay & Co., 750 3rd Ave., NY, NY

Folk Harps, Gildas Jaffrennou, Model & Allied Publications Ltd., Book Division, Station Rd., Kings Langley, Herts., England

Drawings of Musical Instruments, Division of Musical Instruments, National Museum of History and Technology, Smithsonian Institution, Washington, D.C. 20560

Making Musical Instruments, Irving Sloane, E.P. Dutton, 2 Park Avenue, NY, NY 10016

Instrument Making for Children and Teachers

Musical Instruments (Teaching Primary Science), Dorothy Diamond and Robert Tiffin, Macdonald Educational, 850 Seventh Ave., NY, NY 10019

Whistles and Strings (Teachers Guide), Webster Division, McGraw-Hill Book Co., Manchester Rd., Manchester, Mo 63011

Cornstalk Fiddle and Other Homemade Instruments, Dallas Cline, Oak Publications, 33 West 60th St., NY, NY 10023

Simple Folk Instruments To Make and To Play, Hunter and Judson, Simon & Schuster, 1230 Avenue of the Americas, NY, NY 10020

American Folk Toys—How To Make Them, Dick Schnacke, Penguin Books, Baltimore, Md

More Books about Instruments

Musical Instruments in Color, Peter Gammond, MacMillan Publishing Co., Inc., Riverside, NJ 1975

The History of Musical Instruments, Curt Sachs, W.W. Norton & Co., New York, 1940

Old Musical Instruments, Rene Clemencic, Weidenfeld & Nicolson, 5 Winsley St., London, England

Instruments of the Middle Ages and Renaissance, David Munrow, Oxford University Press, England, 1976

The World of Medieval & Renaissance Musical Instruments, Jeremy Montagu, The Overlook Press, Woodstock, NY, 1976

The World of Musical Instruments, Alan Kendall, Hamlyn Press, New York, 1972

From the Hunter's Bow, Beatrice Edgerly, G.P. Putnam's Sons, East Rutherford, NJ, 1942

European & American Musical Instruments, Anthony Baines, B.T. Batsford Ltd., London, England, 1966

Musical Instruments—A Comprehensive Dictionary, Sibyl Marcuse, W.W. Norton & Co., NY, NY 1964

Musical Instruments of the World—Illustrated Encyclopedia, The Diagram Group, Paddington Press, Ltd., Random House, NY, 1976

Musical Instruments of Africa, Betty Warner Dietz, Michael Olatunji, John Day Co., dist. Harper and Row Pubs., Scranton, PA

The Hill Collection of Musical Instruments, David D. Boyden, Oxford University Press, England, 1969

Genesis of a Music, Harry Partch, DaCapo Press, NY 1973

Horns, Strings, and Harmony, Arthur Benade, Doubleday, N.Y., N.Y.

Inexpensive and Free Literature

Divisions of Musical Instruments, National Museum of History and Technology, Smithsonian Institution, Washington, D.C. 20560

Woodworking Catalogues

Brookestone Co., Dept. C, Brookestone Bldg. Peterborough, NH 83458
A Variety of hard-to-find and unusual tools

Frog Tool Co., Dept. L, 548 N. Wells, St., Chicago, Ill 60610. Power and hand tools.

Garrett-Wade Co., Dept. FW-9-77, 302 Fifth Ave., NY, NY 10001. Fine tools and information.

Sculpture House, Inc., 38 E. 30th St., NY, NY 10016. Woodcarving tools.

Woodcraft Supply Corp., 313 Montvale Ave., Woburn, MA. 01801. Fine selection of all sorts of woodworking tools and some wood.

Woodworkers Supply, P.O. Box 14117, 11200 Menaul N.E., Albuquerque, NM 87112. Wide selection of fine tools.

Lee Valley Tools, 875 Boyd Ave., Ottawa, Canada K2A 2C9

Other Interesting Catalogues

Lark in the Morning, P.O. Box 1176, Mendocino, CA 95460. Packed full of available unusual and exotic instruments.

Bucks County Folk Music Shop, 40 Sand Rd., New Britain, PA 18901. Instrument making accessories, buying, and playing tips.

Mandolin Bros., Ltd., 629 Forest Ave., Staten Island, NY 10310. Clearing house of fine stringed instruments.

Guitars Friend, Rte. 1 Box 200C Sandpoint, Idaho 83864. Wide variety of folk instruments and accessories.

Deiro's Music Headquarters, 133 Seventh Ave., NY, NY 10014. Harps, bagpipes, etc.

B & G Instrument Workshop, 318 North 36th St., Seattle, WA 98103. For all your string needs. Harpsichord specialists. Good selection of music wire.

Elderly Instruments, 541 E. Grand River, East Lansing, Michigan. Highly recommended.

Periodicals

Banjo Newsletter, 1301 Hawkins Lane, Annapolis, Md 21401. What's what in banjoland.

Dulcimer Players News, Philip Mason, RFD 2, Box 132, Bangor, ME 04401. For the dulcimaniacs.

Mandolin Notebook, 12704 Barbara Rd., Silver Spring, Md 20906. All you need to know about mandolins.

Mugwumps Instrument Herald, 12704 Barbara Rd., Silver Spring, Md 20906. A must if you're interested in folk instruments.

Fine Woodworking, The Taunton Press, P.O. Box 355, Newton, CT. An incredible source of inspiration and information for the serious woodworker.

Pickin', North American Bldg., 401 N. Broad St., Phila.,

PA 19108. The latest on folk music of all types.

Sing Out!, 270 Lafayette St., NY, NY 10012. A Good folk song magazine.

"Canada Folk" Bulletin, Room 101-337 Carrall St., Vancouver, BC V6B 2J4. Perspectives on what's happening where in Canada.

Folk Harp Journal, P.O. Box 161, Mt. Laguna, CA 92048. The folk harp—its construction, its music, and the techniques of its use.

Music Information Books

Music of the Whole Earth, David Reck, Charles Scribner's Sons, NY, NY

Dulcimer People, Jean Ritchie, Oak Publications, 33 W. 60th St., NY, NY 10023

The Mountain Dulcimer: How to Make It and Play It, Howie Mitchell, Folk-Legacy Records, Inc., Sharon, CT 06069

The Hammered Dulcimer, Howie Mitchell, Folk-Legacy Records, Inc., Sharon, CT 06069

The Hammered Dulcimer Compendium, Mugwumps, 12704 Barbara Rd., Silver Spring, Md 20906

The Folk Music Sourcebook, Oak Publications, 33 West 60th St., N.Y., N.Y. 10023

The Irish Harp, Joan Rimmer, Mercier Press, 4 Bridge St., Cork, Ireland

Violin Making As It Was and Is, Heron-Allen, Ward Lock Limited, 116 Baker St., London, England

The Irish and Highland Harps, Robert Armstrong, Salvi Publications, International Harp Corporation, 1649 Tenth St., Santa Barbara, CA 90404

GLOSSARY

Backsaw   A fine-toothed rectangular saw that has extra reinforcing along the back of the blade. Used for fine cuts.

Bandsaw   An electric saw characterized by a continuous thin blade in the form of a loop.

Bass bar   A long narrow piece of softwood glued into many bowed instruments to help transfer vibrations and reinforce the soundboard.

Bottleneck   A glass or metal "noter" (sometimes broken neck from bottle) used to slide along strings for special effect.

Brace and bit   A boring tool having a crank (brace) which holds a drill or auger (bit).

Bridge   A piece of wood that helps transmit vibrations to the sound box on stringed instruments. Also delineates a specific string length.

Chordophone   A musical instrument having strings as tone-producing elements.

Concert pitch   A standard pitch by which European and North American musicians gauge their tuning.

Coping saw   A saw with a narrow blade set in an open frame used to cut curves.

Diatonic scale   A standard scale of eight notes to the octave with no chromatic intervals.

Dovetail saw   A small fine-toothed back saw for small accurate cuts.

Dremel tool   A small hobbyist's router.

End block   A block of wood usually found at the end of the sound box which stabilizes the top, sides, and back.

Fingerboard   The area of a stringed instrument along which notes are stopped with the fingers.

Flue hole   The sound-producing hole found in recorder type instruments.

Fret wire   Small metal bars arranged across the fingerboard of many stringed instruments delineating a specific scale.

Fretsaw   A fine-blade saw with a deep open frame used to cut small curves and scroll work. Also a saw used to cut fret slots.

Friction pegs   Violin style pegs tapered to fit tightly in a hole.

Froe   A woodworking tool used to split segments of logs.

Forepillar   The supporting member of a harp found opposite the sound box.

Glissando   A fast pattern or sweep of notes. Sliding up and down a scale.

Grommet   A metal eyelet or ring to reinforce holes.

Gut string   Music string made from the sinew of animals.

Hacksaw   A fine-toothed saw with an open frame specifically designed to cut metal.

Hardwood   Wood derived from deciduous or leafy (not evergreen) trees.

Hitch pin   A small pin which anchors the end of a taut string. The other end is usually attached to a tuning mechanism.

Hone   To sharpen on a stone or other fine abrasive material.

Ionian mode   A major diatonic scale in the modal system of tuning first evolved by the Greeks.

Jigsaw   Tool designed to cut ornate or curved patterns and designs in relatively thin pieces of wood.

Jointer   Tool designed to smooth and level medium-size lengths of wood.

Jug band   Musical group characterized by use of home implements for instruments.

Keyhole saw   A long pointed tablesaw used to cut interior holes.

Luthier   Literally, a lute maker. Generally, a maker of fine musical instruments.

Machine tuner   A geared tuning device found on many stringed instruments (especially guitar).

Mallets   Percussion sticks used for striking strings, drums, and other percussion instruments.

Modal   A system of scales evolved by the Greeks which gave each scale a particular tonality or feeling.

Mortise   A hollowed-out space in a piece of wood into which a corresponding projection fits forming a joint.

Nodal point   A point on a vibrating object (string or bar) where the least vibration takes place.

Noter   A stick or dowel held in the left hand to facilitate a melody. Used instead of the fingers.

Nut   A small piece of hardwood that runs at right angles to the strings to help delineate the string length of an instrument.

Octave   A span of eight notes. Each octave doubles (or halves) the number of vibrations per second.

Peg head   The end of a stringed instrument to which the tuning mechanisms are attached.

Perfect fifth (sol-do)   A significant and strong harmonic interval in Western music.

Pick   A flexible plectrum used to enhance the sound of plucked strings.

Pin block   A piece of hardwood in which tuning pins are seated.

Pitch   The subjective term for vibrations per second.

Pot   A resonating chamber on a banjo.

Psaltery   A plucked zither known from Medieval times on.

Radial arm saw   An electric saw used primarily for cross cutting wood.

Rat-tail file   A round tapered file.

Rasp   A coarse file.

Reamer   A tool with sharp edges for enlarging or tapering a hole.

Resaw   To saw wood planks into thinner slabs. Cutting wood on edge.

Resonator   A hollow air-filled cavity on instruments which helps amplify the sound.

Rhythm   A regular repetition of sound, beat, or movement.

Router   A tool which removes small areas of wood.

Scale   Any fixed set of tones having certain intervals between them.

Skiptooth blade   A blade with extra spacing between the teeth for sawing hard-to-cut materials.

Sound box   An enclosed body of air which reinforces and amplifies the sound of an instrument.

Sound hole   A decorative and functional hole in the sound box.

Sound waves   A sequence of compressions and refractions caused by molecular movement of the air is caused by a vibrating object.

Soundboard   That part of an instrument most responsible for increasing the vibrating area thus amplifying the sound.

Soundpost   A softwood post set in some bowed instruments to transfer vibration between the top and back. Also helps support the pressure of the strings on the soundboard.

Spokeshave   A type of hand plane with handles on both sides useful for planing curved surfaces.

String rib   A reinforcing strip for the strings found down the center of the soundboard in a harp.

Strum   A rapid movement of the hand across the strings of an instrument.

Strum hollow   An area on an Appalachian Mountain dulcimer where picking and strumming are usually done.

Syncopation   An "offbeat" rhythm. A rhythm that reinforces the weak beats in a measure of time.

Tablesaw   An electric woodworking saw especially designed to cut lengths of lumber (rip cut).

Template   A cut-out pattern used for design transfer.

Tenon   A tongue of wood cut so that it will fit into a hole of another piece forming a joint.

Timbre   Tone quality.

Tine of a fret   That portion of a fret that fits tightly into a fine slot cut on the fingerboard thus holding it in place.

Toggles   A crosspiece attached to a rope or string to help tighten a drum head.

Tuner   A mechanism by which the pitch of a string can be changed.

Tuning pin   A pin designed to be turned by an accompanying wrench to loosen and tighten strings on an instrument.

Tuning wrench   A device used to grip a tuning pin in socket fashion.

Veneer   Very thin slabs of wood.

Whetstone   A very hard stone used for sharpening metal blades.

Zither   Any stringed instrument which has strings stretched from end to end or side to side.

Zither pins   Tuning pins of a certain size and shape designed for use on zithers.

Acknowledgments

This book is a new and refined edition of *Making Folk Instruments in Wood* published in 1987.

My gratitude to Vilnis Vulfs and The Woodworks who first introduced me to woodworking. Thereafter, David Square, Steve Hunter, Drew Pastuck, John Wiznuk, Ilka Salo, Donovan Timmers, and Glenn Barney proved that we could cooperatively pursue our craft and survive. Thanks also to Lorraine Sutton, Chuck McCandliss, Mitch Padolak, Paul Lewis, the Winnipeg Folklore Center, the Manitoba Arts Council, and many others for supporting the cause of handmade instruments and homegrown music. Special thanks to Larry Fisher, master harp maker, musician, and folklorist, who continues the tradition of instrument making in Winnipeg and across Canada.

During my pursuit of a doctoral degree in ethnomusicology at Wesleyan University in Connecticut, my interest in and knowledge of music and folk instruments grew and diversified. Thanks to David McAllester, Fred Stubbs, Carol Worden, Tom Randall, David Cross, the Connecticut Commission on the Arts, and Allison Spitzer's Bright Solutions for their help. Giovanni Ciarlo and Kathleen Sartor, aka Sirius Coyote, added to my musical and instrumental enrichment. Appreciation also to Gregory Acker for xylophone ideas, Peter Hadley for digeridoo information, and Kristen Dockendorff for insights for clay whistles and ocarinas. And final thanks to David Magnuson, who assisted through the extensive process of rebuilding and refining scores of instruments; this edition would not have been possible without his enthusiasm and support.

And thanks to the children and adults who participated in playing the instruments for photography: Don and Catherine Shankweiler; Edmund and Theresa Viner; Nan, Matthew, Hanna, and Bram Kyer; Krista and Noah Rappahahn; David, Sarah, Jason, and Miriam Magnuson; Michelle, Megan, Samantha, and Jeremy McGeowan; Mark and Gus Giangrave; Cindy Larsen; Tasha Millikan; Ethyl Poindexter

126

About the Author

Dennis G. Waring is an ethnomusicologist, educational consultant, musician, and instrument maker. Dr. Waring teaches American Music, World Music, and Music Education; conducts educational workshops and institutes nationally; and performs extensively in the public sector.

INDEX